DAILY DEVOTIONS

Alive 2

DAILY DEVOTIONS

S. Rickly Christian

ZondervanPublishingHouse

Grand Rapids, Michigan

A Division of HarperCollinsPublishers

Alive 2
Copyright © 1983, 1995 by S. Rickly Christian

Requests for information should be addressed to:

⬛ ZondervanPublishingHouse
Grand Rapids, Michigan 49530

Library of Congress Cataloging-in-Publication Data

Christian, S. Rickly (Scott Rickly)
    Alive 2 : daily devotions / S. Rickly Christian.
        p.   cm.
    ISBN: 0-310-49911-9
    1. Teenagers—Prayer-books and devotions—English. 2. Devotional calendars.
I. Title.
BV4850.C533   1995
242.63—dc 20   95-19414
                                                 CIP
                                                 AC

Interior photos on pages 115, 129, 165, 177, 189, 239, and 313 by H. Armstrong Roberts, Inc. All other interior photos by Cleo Freelance Photography.

Cover design by Paula Gibson
Interior design by Sue Koppenol

Printed in the United States of America

For My Parents

Even youths grow tired and weary,
and young men stumble and fall;
but those who hope in the Lord
will renew their strength.
They will soar on wings like eagles;
they will run and not grow weary,
they will walk and not be faint.

Isaiah 40:30–31

CONTENTS

INTRODUCTION

When you have more pressure in your day than hours, it's easy for God to get lost in the squeeze. We all have our moments when it's difficult to *connect* with him in some meaningful way. After all, he doesn't exactly maintain a high profile. When was the last time *you* saw him?

I'd do something about that if I were God. I wouldn't be so shy. Perhaps God could learn from the way they start football games at the Air Force Academy in Colorado Springs. A half dozen or so young cadets bail out of a plane circling overhead and parachute onto the fifty yard line of the field. The refs, the players, and the fans all peer skyward to watch the cadets' descent, and for good reason. The game can't begin until the last parachutist lands, because he carries the game ball. As the ball is passed to the ref, the crowd roars, and then jet fighters scream overhead, slam on their afterburners, and rocket straight up and out of sight. It's enough to make you wet your pants.

I think that's how I'd do it if I were God, except I wouldn't use a parachute and I wouldn't land. I'd free-fall headfirst, and then pull up into a hover just at the top of the stadium. I'd do the jet thing, but would catch them in midair, one in each hand. And then I'd let rip a few lightning bolts just to let people know it was really me, and boom out something like, "I am the Lord your God, and you shall worship me!"

Concerns about God's low visibility are nothing new. Throughout the Bible, people constantly ask why he keeps his distance or inquire where to find him. The Bible doesn't fully explain why God doesn't make a bigger deal about being God, but I suspect it's largely out of respect for us. He holds back because he knows we can handle only so much reality at a time. And so he reveals himself in brief, people-sized glimpses.

You might see these glimpses in the colorful splash of sunset, the promise of spring, the comfort of his Holy Spirit. You might see them in an everyday kindness somebody shows you, the humor of a snail's face, the assurance of forgiveness. You hopefully see these glimpses sometimes when you look at yourself in the mirror—the miracle of a changed life.

Think of what you read in this book (and its companion volume, *Alive 1*) as glimpses of God. They provide quick snapshots of God in everyday life, and show his concern and love for you in the midst of everything you face in your teen years—your happy young-and-crazy times, your tentative try-and-be-cool times, your wide-grinned best of times, or your gut-wrenching worst of times.

These daily glimpses essentially convey the message that God didn't just visit Planet Earth long ago and then retreat to some distant corner of the universe, leaving you to struggle and stumble through life on your own. He's there beside you, every step of the way.

S. Rickly Christian
Colorado Springs, Colorado

WEEK 1

GETTING PERSONAL

> *Because you are sons, God sent the Spirit of his*
> *Son into our hearts, the Spirit who calls out, "Abba,*
> *Father." So you are no longer a slave, but a son; and since*
> *you are a son, God has made you also an heir.*
>
> GALATIANS 4:6–7

Like most parents, mine laid down a few basic rules for our house. The short list was the essence of what they considered to be good manners.

Among their rules: Don't burp at the table; don't pick your nose in public (or anywhere else, for that matter); don't spit on the sidewalk; don't hit girls; and don't chew with your mouth open. There was another rule, in a class by itself: Don't call adults by their first names.

No problem if my parents called their best friends Ken and Eleanor. But it was World War III if I called them anything but *Mr.* and *Mrs.* Elbert. The formality indicated respect for elders, they said. So the man who delivered bottled water to our house was always *Mr.* Griffith to me, and the mechanic who fixed the car was nothing but *Mr.* Russell.

The only adults I could address like normal human beings were my parents. With them, just plain old Mom and Dad was fine.

When Moses was first confronted face to face by God in Exodus 3, he wasn't quite sure how to address him. He realized the holiness of God demanded something formal, but *Mr. God* probably didn't sound quite right. So he asked God what he should call him, and God suggested he use the name *Yahweh*. That divine name, derived from the Hebrew verb *to be*, roughly means "I am who I am."

Yahweh was primarily used by the high priest on special occasions, because people believed it was too holy to be spoken by just anybody. Ordinary Joes called God *Adonai*, which means Lord, and *Sabaoth* or *Shaddai*, which can be translated as

Almighty. As names go, they're still quite formal. But what do you expect with God?

And then, all of a sudden, things changed. Jesus arrived on the face of the earth. He called God by a new name: *Abba*, which in Aramaic means Daddy. It shook some people up, because God was supposed to be distant, untouchable, unapproachable. "Daddy" was just too personal—a name that sons and daughters called their very own fathers!

They missed the point by a country mile. It was for that very reason that "Daddy" was just fine.

See also: Exodus 3:11–14; Mark 14:36; Romans 8:15–17

NICKNAMES

He appointed twelve–designating them apostles– that they might be with him and that he might send them out to preach and to have authority to drive out demons. These are the twelve he appointed: Simon (to whom he gave the name Peter); James son of Zebedee, and his brother John (to them he gave the name Boanerges, which means Sons of Thunder); Andrew, Philip, Bartholomew, Matthew, Thomas, James son of Alphaeus, Thaddaeus, Simon the Zealot and Judas Iscariot, who betrayed him.

MARK 3:14–19

Close friends often have nicknames for each other. They call each other strange names that otherwise might prompt a fistfight. Silly though they are, names like Noodles, Scooter, Thumper, Flash, or Tiny are actually indicative of extreme affection. One of my best friends, who has a dime-sized mole on his cheek, goes by Nathan to most people. I sometimes call him Spot.

The use of such abbreviated names was common in Bible days. Take, for example, James and John, two of Jesus' closest companions. When these hotheaded brothers once suggested they'd like to nuke a lousy welcoming committee in Samaria (Luke 9:51–56), Jesus nicknamed them Sons of Thunder. They probably smiled every time they heard him calling them.

Then there were the two Simons. Jesus referred to one as The Zealot and affectionately rechristened the other one Peter, a nickname that, humorously enough, means "The Rock." Peter was, after all, somewhat stone-brained on occasion. And a rock is pretty basic; there's nothing too fancy or pretty about it. But in God's creation, barring an earthquake, a rock is about as solid as anything you can find. And when the going got tough, Peter was rock solid.

There's something both touching and very ... well, *human* about this aspect of Jesus' life as reflected in this simple listing of his friends' nicknames. You get the idea that personal relationships really meant something special to him.

In that regard, things really haven't changed much in two thousand years.

See also: John 15:9–17; Romans 5:7–11

NAME CALLING

Today, if you hear his voice, do not harden your hearts.

HEBREWS 4:7

Moving through the crowded locker hall, your mind is already on the weekend. Oblivious to oncoming traffic, you're thinking Saturday night even though you're smack in the middle of another ordinary week.

Suddenly you hear your name. Your brain whirs back to the present. You stop, turn, and expectantly scan the nearby faces. And then you spot a good friend, beckoning from across the hallway, and feel a smile starting to spread.

It's a simple pleasure, hearing your name called out in a crowd. It creates a sense of expectancy, of anticipation. Suddenly, you're not just another anonymous, milling face. You have been noticed.

Zacchaeus probably felt that way the day Jesus passed through Jericho. A near-anonymous man whose name is mentioned just once in the New Testament (Luke 19:1–10), he was, in blunt terms, a crook—a legman for the Roman IRS who, if living today, would wear his shirt open to his navel and have three pounds of gold chains dangling from his neck. In addition to being a shyster, Zacchaeus was vertically challenged—something of a legal dwarf. So when the crowd began milling around Jesus, Zacchaeus shinnied up a tree for a better view.

That's when he got the surprise of his life. Through the roar of the crowd, he suddenly heard his name being called. When he turned around in the branches and saw it was Jesus beckoning him, Zacchaeus probably fell out of the tree in astonishment. It's a wonder he didn't suffer a coronary too, because in the next breath Jesus said, "I *must* stay at your house today!"

What could he make of it? What can anybody make of it other than the fact that, for reasons known only to him, God seems to have similar plans for every last peculiar one of us. "I must stay with *you!*"

The only hitch is that you must first cock an ear toward heaven and, above the drone of the humdrum, listen for his still small voice calling your name.

See also: Psalm 46:10; 2 Thessalonians 1:11; Revelation 3:20

A NAME YOU CAN COUNT ON

He who overcomes will . . . be dressed in white. I will never erase his name from the book of life, but will acknowledge his name before my Father and his angels.

REVELATION 3:5

I've become used to being identified by long strings of numbers.

To the feds, I am known by a nine-digit Social Security number. By dialing another number, an eleven-digit sequence (including the prefix 1), anybody in the world can talk directly with me. The bank computer recognizes me by a personal access code, which I can use to withdraw cash from my account at 3 A.M. if I'm so inclined. Since the code is secret, my kid brother is prevented from doing the same if he's likewise so inclined.

I've also got a license plate number that the Department of Motor Vehicles uses to identify me. And to *Time* magazine, I am not Rick Christian, but a file number of twenty-seven letters and digits, CRIMU603S94T591107JUL87CA51. With *Campus Life* magazine, I am 000100769299CLJUL873937.

There are, of course, good reasons why numeric codes are used. They enable you to single out a particular John Smith from all the other billions of funny-looking, two-legged creatures sharing this planet. This is important, say, if you want to send him a parking ticket, or telephone him to whisper sweet nothings in his ear.

Nevertheless, I rather like it when I'm waiting for a haircut or a table at a restaurant, and I hear my *name* being called. And when Luke writes, "Rejoice that your names are written in heaven," I am overcome by one of those stand-up-and-holler kind of feelings.

It reminds me that I'm not just an insignificant blip or a twenty-seven-digit code in some dusty memory bank of the universe.

Rather, my name (*my* name!) is carved into the Book of Life. Pure and simple, my salvation is guaranteed in writing.

And on that day when I join my Lord in heaven, I expect he'll be waiting for me at the gates with his arms open wide and my name on his lips.

See also: Psalm 69:27–28; Daniel 12:1–2; Luke 10:20; Philippians 4:3; Hebrews 12:22–23

TOO CLOSE FOR COMFORT

You will receive power when the Holy Spirit comes on you; and you will be my witnesses in Jerusalem, and in all Judea and Samaria, and to the ends of the earth.

ACTS 1:8

In the Bible, God put a premium on developing close personal relationships. We're told he walked through the Garden with Adam and Eve. He appeared before Moses and revealed his name. Housed in the temple, he dwelt among the Israelites.

But not even that was personal enough. He wanted to establish a closer relationship. And so, for reasons best known only to himself, he became one of us for thirty-three years.

For some people, his visit was thirty-three years too long. Many just felt too uncomfortable with him around. Jesus challenged what they said and how they lived. Friday nights weren't the same with the Son of God liable to walk around the corner at any moment.

So they took matters into their own hands and nailed him to a cross. God's first-degree love prompted first-degree punishment. And when Christ breathed his last, his executioners thought they could get back to business as usual. They had, of course, underestimated the depth of God's love—and the power of it. His love simply wouldn't die that Friday at Calvary. It was like trying to blow out a trick candle. They huffed and puffed and did everything they were supposed to do, but then a tiny spark suddenly flashed through the smoke, a flame sputtered, and before they knew it some crazy women were saying the king of the Jews had risen. Imagine! The age-old dictum, "Where there's smoke, there's fire," proved to be true.

The flame, fanned by whatever happens to people when they see somebody rise from the dead, spread from house to house. It whipped through the docks, the synagogues, the prisons. The whole city and beyond was engulfed by the wildfire.

Even now, all these years later, if you step outside and sniff ever so gently, you can still smell the smoke. Take a deep breath. Something's burning. It's a thing called love.

See also: Psalm 104:4; John 20:1–18; Acts 2:1–4

THE DEEPEST FRIENDS

The thief comes only to steal and kill and destroy;
I have come that they may have life, and have it to the full.
I am the good shepherd. The good shepherd lays down his
life for the sheep.

JOHN 10:10–11

Some of my most cherished possessions are my school yearbooks. If my house ever caught fire, they'd be among the first things I'd grab as I ran outside. Penned in various colors of ink throughout the annuals are entries such as this:

Dear Rick, Your friendship means the world to me, and I'll never forget you or the times we shared. Love, Diana.

On adjacent pages are dozens of other entries, signed by other good friends: Helen, Sam, Donna, Jerry, Anita, Mark, Cyndee, and many others. Just seeing my friends' names is enough to flood my mind with endless memories of first loves, broken romances, cruddy jobs, smelly gym clothes, and Friday night football games. Their names conjure to my mind a unique blend of hilarity and agony, accomplishments and embarrassments, bravado and desperado. Though most of us went our separate ways after graduation, I'll never forget the bunch of them.

Take a minute and think about those people who have had the biggest impact on your life. What are their names, and what do you think of when you think of them? Go ahead, forget about everything else going on around you. Filter out distractions and just drift mentally for a few minutes. Take five, slip your brain into neutral, and focus on two or three of their names.

If you're anything like me, it's impossible to think of anybody's name without also picturing that person's face. And once a person's face is on my mental screen, I am barraged by movie-like sequences. It's as if all during our friendship a little hidden camera had been shooting video to be stored in my head for later playback.

Certain names and faces make you laugh out loud as you recall some hilariously nonsensical moment you shared. Remember the dumb jokes? The sound of that friend's giggle? How another friend's eyes crinkled up at the corners? The video is perfectly intact in your mind.

Of course, not all memories are happy. A broken friendship is among the worst tragedies in the world. And if a good friend has died or moved away, the thought of his or her name can bring tears. That's exactly what happened when Jesus was told his good friend Lazarus had died. No little sniffle; he wept (John 11:35). His buddy was dead, and Jesus felt the loss clear to his bones. That's true of all good friends. The more you care, the more it can hurt in the end.

Friendship was serious business with Christ. When his friends were hurting, he healed them. When they were hungry, he fed them. When they were discouraged, he prayed with them. And when they were dying, he cried for them.

Of course, it wasn't enough that he shed tears. He knew it would take blood. And so he said, "Greater love has no one than this, that one lay down his life for his friends." Shortly thereafter, at a place called Calvary, he put his life on the line for his friends.

The world hasn't gotten over it yet.

See also: John 15:13; Romans 5:7–8; Philippians 2:5–11

POINTS TO PONDER: FRIENDSHIP

I have called you friends, for everything that I learned from my Father I have made known to you.

JOHN 15:15

Not many sounds in life, and I include all urban and all rural sounds, exceed in interest a knock at the door.

CHARLES LAMB

Fellowship is heaven, and lack of fellowship is hell.

WILLIAM MORRIS

It is possible to be still enough to enjoy companionship with God.

J. GUSTAV WHITE

Bad company is the devil's net.

ANONYMOUS

The only way to have a friend is to be one.

RALPH WALDO EMERSON

I am to become a Christ to my neighbor and be for him what Christ is for me.

MARTIN LUTHER

Alas, my God, that we should be
Such strangers to each other!
O that as friends we might agree,
And walk and talk together.

THOMAS SHEPHERD

Friendship is one mind in two bodies.

MENCIUS

Thy friendship oft has made my heart to ache; do be my enemy—
for friendship's sake.

WILLIAM BLAKE

I never found the companion that was so companionable as solitude.

HENRY DAVID THOREAU

I never met a man I didn't like.

WILL ROGERS

Friendship without self-interest is one of the rare and beautiful
things of life.

JAMES FRANCIS BYRNES

You can make more friends in two months by becoming really
interested in other people than you can make in two years by trying to get people interested in you.

DALE CARNEGIE

It is easier to love humanity than to befriend the new kid who
moved to town from Guam.

S. RICKLY CHRISTIAN

The firmest friendships have been formed in mutual adversity, as
iron is most strongly united by the fiercest flame.

CHARLES C. COLTON

Friendship is something that raised us almost above humanity. This love, free from instinct, free from all duties but those which love has freely assumed, almost wholly free from jealousy, and free without qualification from the need to be needed, is eminently spiritual. It is the sort of love one can imagine between angels.

C. S. LEWIS

Promises may get friends, but it is performance that keeps them.

OWEN FELTHAM

Jesus' home was the road along which he walked with his friends in search of new friends.

GIOVANNI PAPINI

After the friendship of God, a friend's affection is the greatest treasure here below.

ANONYMOUS

How can I lift a struggling soul and guide him if I never take his arm?

VIOLA JACOBSON BERG

I loved the talk, the laughter, the courteous little gestures toward one another, the sharing of the study of books of eloquence, the companionship that was sometimes serious and sometimes hilariously nonsensical, the differences of opinion that left no more bad feeling than if a man were disagreeing with his own self, the rare disputes that simply seasoned the normal consensus of agreement.

AUGUSTINE OF HIPPO

In misery it is great comfort to have a companion.

JOHN LYLY

See also: Proverbs 18:24; Luke 7:34; James 2:21–23; 4:4

WEEK 2

A TWO-LETTER ANSWER

How long, O Lord, must I call for help, but you do not listen?

HABAKKUK 1:2

Dear God, she's beautiful. We met last week in history, and I knew at first glance we'd hit it off. I could tell the match was made in heaven. After all, she was a strong Christian and had the best legs on campus. So why did she say no when I asked her out? I'd prayed about it and everything....

Dear God, it's only my future. From day one, everybody's called me Shakespeare and acted as if everything I write is Pulitzer material. With that kind of encouragement, I was naturally thinking I'd get a journalism degree and then hitch up with a large metro daily or maybe even write a book. All the details were in place, and I even got a job to cover j-school tuition. So why was my application rejected? I'd prayed about it and everything....

Like it or not, prayers often don't get answered the way we'd like. God doesn't always say *yes.* Sometimes his answer is *wait.* Quite often it is *no.*

King David once prayed nonstop for a week that his son's life would be spared. On the seventh day, the child died. Another time, the prophet Elijah asked God to end his life. But when he opened his eyes, he was still very much alive. Then there's the apostle Paul, who desperately wanted to take a missionary journey to Asia. God sent him to Europe instead. And three times he asked God to remove his thorn in the flesh. Three times he heard God's answer: "No. No. NO!"

Not to forget the time when, shortly before his crucifixion, Jesus prayed, "Father, if you are willing, take this cup from me." His Father wasn't willing; Plan B wasn't good enough. It would take the cross to save the world.

In cases where we get something other than what we want, we tend to become moody. Sometimes we cry and carry on. However, if we were smart enough to know better, we'd turn cartwheels when God responds to our prayers with a short, two-letter answer.

No is a sign that God has something far better in mind for us than we, from our limited perspective, could have possibly imagined. *No* should be good news. It's when we continually get what we want that we ought to be concerned.

See also: 2 Samuel 12:15–19; 1 Kings 19:3–18; Luke 22:39–44; 2 Corinthians 12:7–10

A YOUNG GIRL STILL DWELLS

The King will say ... "I was hungry and you gave me something to eat, I was thirsty and you gave me something to drink, I was a stranger and you invited me in, I needed clothes and you clothed me, I was sick and you looked after me, I was in prison and you came to visit me."

Then the righteous will answer him, "Lord, when did we see you hungry and feed you, or thirsty and give you something to drink? When did we see you a stranger and invite you in, or needing clothes and clothe you? When did we see you sick or in prison and go to visit you?" The King will reply, "I tell you the truth, whatever you did for one of the least of these brothers of mine, you did for me."

MATTHEW 25:34–40

The following poem was written by a woman who died in the old folks' ward of Ashludie Hospital near Dundee, England. It was found among her possessions and so impressed the staff that copies were widely distributed throughout the hospital and beyond:

What do you see, nurse, what do you see?
Are you thinking when you look at me—
A crabbed old woman, not very wise,

Uncertain of habit with faraway eyes?
Who dribbles her food and makes no reply
When you say in a loud voice, "I do wish you'd try"
Who seems not to notice the things that you do,
And forever is losing a stocking or shoe?
Who resisting or not, lets you do as you will
With bathing and feeding, the long day to fill?
Is that what you're thinking, is that what you see?
Then open your eyes, nurse, you're looking at me.
I'll tell you who I am as I sit here so still,
As I move at your bidding, eat at your will . . .
I'm a small child of ten with a father and mother,
Brothers and sisters who love one another;
A young girl of sixteen with wings on her feet,
Dreaming that soon a love she'll meet;
A bride at twenty my heart gives a leap,
Remembering the vows that I promised to keep;
At twenty-five now I have young of my own
Who need me to build a secure, happy home;
A woman of thirty, my young now grow fast,
Bound together with ties that should last;
At forty, my young sons have grown up and gone,
But my man's beside me to see I don't mourn;
At fifty, once more babies play round my knee,
Again we know children my loved ones and me.
Dark days are upon me; my husband is dead,
I look at the future, I shudder with dread.
For my young are all rearing young of their own,
And I think of the years and the love that I've known.
I'm an old woman now and nature is cruel;
'Tis her jest to make old age look like a fool.
The body it crumbles, grace and vigor depart;
There is a stone where I once had a heart.
But inside this old carcass a young girl still dwells,

And now, again, my embittered heart swells.
I remember the joys, I remember the pain,
And I'm loving and living life over again.
I think of the years, all too few, gone too fast,
And accept the stark fact that nothing can last.
So open your eyes, nurse, open and see
Not a crabbed old woman,
Look closer—see me!

This poem was intended for those who surrounded the woman in her last days. But there's something about it that reminds me about my own grandparents ... about some of the old people at church that I breeze past without looking them in the eye ... about the old bag lady who paws through our garbage cans on trash days ... about everybody who is somehow different from me, who talks different, looks different or acts different ... and about how Jesus in Matthew 25:35–40 really seems to be saying:

So open your eyes, children, open and see
Not faceless people around you,
Look closer—see me!

See also: Job 31:32; Hebrews 13:1–3; Revelation 20:11–15

TRIVIAL PURSUIT

Do not store up for yourselves treasures on earth,
where moth and rust destroy, and where thieves break in
and steal. But store up for yourselves treasures in heaven,
where moth and rust do not destroy, and where thieves do
not break in and steal. For where your treasure is, there
your heart will be also.

MATTHEW 6:19–21

Stuck away in a deep, very dark corner of my closet is a board game that I'm not very good at and for which I spent too much money. It's called Trivial Pursuit. I generally lose when I play because it's hard for me to remember relatively insignificant information that I never learned in the first place.

To win at Trivial Pursuit, you've got to know answers to such questions as: What's the only mammal that can't jump? Or, What fruit is packed with the most calories? Or, What finger boasts the fastest-growing nail?*

When I draw especially tough questions, which I could never answer in a million years, I often punctuate the silence with loud groans, exasperated sighs, and comments such as: "Wait a sec, the answer is *right* on the tip of my tongue!" When my opponent draws the head-scratchers, I make the exact same noises, but substitute comments such as: "*You* get all the easy questions!" In other words, I'm all bluff.

Exasperating as it is, Trivial Pursuit is an entertaining way to kill a couple of hours. But it's more than just a board game. For many people the name describes the way they live their lives: *trivial pursuit*. We play it whenever we spend our time, our energy, our thoughts in pursuit of trivial matters; whenever we ignore what's really important; whenever we are distracted by things of little consequence.

As such, trivial pursuit is a *Playboy* magazine, the backseat of a parked car, or a snort of coke (even just to *try* it). Trivial pursuit is stumbling along with C's when you know you can get A's, running with the wrong crowd, gossiping behind somebody's back, or eating a second doughnut when you know you shouldn't have eaten the first.

Trivial pursuit says, "I'll love you *if* you'll let me borrow the car; *if* you will go to bed with me" ... or, "*because* you were MVP in last week's game; *because* you have a great body and blonde hair."

Trivial pursuit is a game which many people play every single day of their lives. It's a pursuit after goals and ambitions and things that aren't eternal. And because of that, it's a game nobody ever wins.

*ANSWERS: The elephant, the avocado, and the middle finger.

See also: Proverbs 21:21; John 12:25; Philippians 3:17–21; 1 Timothy 6:11–12

ALMOST ... BUT NOT QUITE

You are not far from the kingdom of God.

MARK 12:34

Almost. It's a sad-sounding, six-letter word that implies a fumbled opportunity, near-miss effort, fizzled dream, close-call decision, botched attempt, missed chance. The word means nearly, just about, not quite.

Almost is the pop fly that would have been caught had the sun not flashed in your eyes; the test that would have been passed had you taken more time to study; the relationship that would have been salvaged had you not lost your temper; the appointment that would have been kept had you not run out of gas.

Almost is the fish that got away; the race lost on a technicality; the election defeat by a single vote.

Almost is the near-win attempt, the second-place finish, the runner-up effort, the foul tip, the misfire.

Almost is college basketball star Len Bias, who captured national headlines when he became the top draft pick by the Boston Celtics and then died days later at his University of Maryland dormitory after he OD'd on cocaine.

Almost is the rich young man (see Mark 10:17–22) who'd kept all the commandments since he was a little boy. But by refusing to sell his possessions and follow Jesus, he made it clear that he was unwilling to put Christ first in his life.

35

Almost is the teacher of the law (see Mark 12:28–34) who could speak fluent Christianese, went to church often enough to be labeled religious, had all the right answers ... but, as far as we know, never made a personal commitment to Jesus Christ. "You are not far from the kingdom of God," Christ told him in the classic understatement of all time.

What the teacher of the law didn't realize was that with Jesus, there's no middle ground. If you're not hot, you're cold. If you're not a saved sinner, you're a damned sinner. *Almost* may count for something in horseshoes and hand grenades. But with Christ, *almost* is a sure ticket to hell.

See also: Lamentations 3:40; Matthew 7:13–14; 1 Corinthians 9:24–27; 2 Corinthians 13:5–6; Revelation 3:15–16

SWITCHING TAGS

For although they knew God, they neither glorified him as God nor gave thanks to him, but their thinking became futile and their foolish hearts were darkened. Although they claimed to be wise, they became fools and exchanged the glory of the immortal God for images made to look like mortal man and birds and animals and reptiles.

ROMANS 1:21–23

I don't know how stores determine the prices of things they sell, but I generally believe they're all too high. Jeans, swimsuits, perfume, candy bars, shoes, automobile tires—each costs more than double what I think it's worth.

To strike back, I once devised a secret plan whereby I'd hang out at one of the big stores at the mall, and when they announced the store would be closing in five minutes, I'd disappear into a quiet corner. My goal was to be locked in the store overnight.

Once the employees had gone home, I'd begin my mischief. I'd switch all the price tags.

As I envisioned it, the store would open the next day as usual. Everything would be the same except for the prices. Nike shoes would cost what handkerchiefs cost the previous day. Tags for CDs would be switched with those for batteries; leather coats with those for electric toothbrushes; tennis rackets with those for ice tongs. A new computer could be had for the price of a set of gym clothes, but paper clips would cost a fortune.

I thought my plan was unique, original, one-of-a-kind. But in one respect, Satan beat me to it. He's confounded us with a false sense of values, whereby we spend staggering sums (of money, time, energy, and emotion) for things that have no lasting value. In this topsy-turvy world, "me first" egoism is more highly esteemed than "you first" altruism, sex has the jump on love, good looks are valued more than a good name, titles rate higher than testimonies, and cheap thrills on Saturday night keep us out of church Sunday morning.

Everywhere you look, price tags have been swapped. The devil's tried to dupe us. Fortunately, the value Christ places on our lives isn't based on appearance or performance. It doesn't matter to him whether we can slam-dunk a basketball, squeeze into a bikini, or memorize Leviticus. He accepts us as we are, without qualification. And just to make sure we don't fall for Satan's bargain basement valuation of ourselves, Jesus put his very life on the line.

The price tag said *Calvary*, and he willingly paid it.

See also: Mark 10:45; Romans 1:25–32; 1 Corinthians 6:19–20; Ephesians 1:7–8; 1 Peter 1:18–21

TROUBLE AHEAD

> *Blessed are you when people insult you, persecute you and falsely say all kinds of evil against you because*

of me. Rejoice and be glad, because great is your reward in heaven, for in the same way they persecuted the prophets who were before you.

MATTHEW 5:11–12

Right from the start he was unwelcome. He was born in a barn because the Bethlehem innkeeper wouldn't give his parents the time of day, let alone a set of clean sheets and a room.

If that wasn't bad enough, as a baby he had a contract placed on his life. Disturbed by Micah's prophecy that a "ruler over Israel" would be born in Bethlehem, King Herod envisioned an overthrow of his kingdom by some thumb-sucking monarch. Though Herod may not have personally believed any of that "religious malarkey," everybody knows it is better to be safe than sorry. So he ordered the slaughter of every boy aged two or under throughout the Bethlehem area.

Christ was, of course, pirated out of the country. And for the rest of his life he was on the run. To those who wanted to follow in his footsteps, he curtly said, "Are you ready to rough it? We're not staying in the best inns, you know" (Luke 9:58 *The Message*). He was jeered at, beat up, ridiculed, spat upon, mocked, and finally killed. He knew it was coming, and he forecast the final curtain to his disciples.

He also warned them not to expect any better treatment themselves. Presumably that includes us, too. "You're blessed when your commitment to God provokes persecution," he said at one point (Matthew 5:10 *The Message*). There's a high cost to be paid if you engage in this bitter match against sin. There are no loopholes; every Christian is at risk. As Paul wrote to Timothy: "Anyone who wants to live all out for Christ is in for a lot of trouble; there's no getting around it" (2 Timothy 3:12 *The Message*).

As a general rule, people aren't harmed for acts of kindness. But let that kindness be done in the name of Jesus, and sparks will fly. In some countries, even today, Christians languish in prison. Some are tortured; others have their brains blown out. But in the western world, persecution merely means being laughed at or having doors closed in your face. You may lose a friend or two. Perhaps your parents will prevent you from going to church or weeknight Bible studies. If you live in places such as San Diego or Omaha or London or Frankfurt, chances are it won't get any tougher.

But if persecution *did* involve more than that, and if you *could* be arrested for being a Christian, it would be nice to think the district attorney could file charges that would stick: *He was overheard talking to another student about Christ,* or *She was observed making regular visits to the old folks' home.*

What about it? Would there be enough evidence to convict *you?*

See also: John 15:18–21; 16:1–4; Hebrews 10:32–39; 12:1–11

POINTS TO PONDER: ADVERSITY

Blessed is the man who perseveres under trial, because when he has stood the test, he will receive the crown of life that God has promised to those who love him.

JAMES 1:12

I don't envy those who have never known any pain, physical or spiritual, because I strongly suspect that the capacity for pain and the capacity for joy are equal. Only those who have suffered great pain are able to know equally great joy.

MADELEINE L'ENGLE

Pain is life—the sharper, the more evidence of life.

CHARLES LAMB

When you're up to your waist in alligators, it's difficult to remember that your main objective was to drain the swamp.

ANONYMOUS

Suffering is the seed from which compassion grows.

DOLORES E. MCGUIRE

Our lives have become so antiseptic that we honestly believe we've suffered adversity and experienced affliction if our shoes pinch our toes, if our car is in the shop and we must take the bus, or if we find a bug in our water glass. Meanwhile, much of the world's population can't afford shoes, travel only where they can get by foot, and often die for lack of food and water.

S. RICKLY CHRISTIAN

I have suffered too much in this world not to hope for another.

JEAN JACQUES ROUSSEAU

He knows not his own strength that hath not met adversity. Heaven prepares good men with crosses.

BEN JONSON

If you suffer, thank God! It is a sure sign that you are alive.

ELBERT HUBBARD

Pain adds rest unto pleasure, and teaches the luxury of health.

MARTIN F. TUPPER

Modern man experiences salvation through Christ's suffering, but runs for the medicine cabinet at the first hint of a headache.

S. RICKLY CHRISTIAN

Shut out suffering, and you see only one side of this strange and fearful thing, the life of man. Brightness and happiness and rest— It is only one side of life. Christ saw both sides.

F. W. ROBERTSON

No person is more unhappy than the one who is never in adversity; the greatest affliction of life is never to be afflicted.

ANONYMOUS

Prosperity is a great teacher; adversity is a greater. Possession pampers the mind; privation trains and strengthens it.

WILLIAM HAZLITT

The gem cannot be polished without friction, nor man perfected without trials.

CHINESE PROVERB

I thank God for my handicaps, for through them, I have found myself, my work and my God.

HELEN KELLER

Affliction comes to us not to make us sad but sober; not to make us sorry but wise.

HENRY WARD BEECHER

It is remarkable with what Christian fortitude and resignation we can bear the suffering of other folks.

JONATHAN SWIFT

Though all afflictions are evils in themselves, yet they are good for us, because they discover to us our disease and tend to our cure.

JOHN TILLOTSON

Affliction, like the iron-smith, shapes as it smites.

CHRISTIAN NESTELL BOVEE

See also: 2 Corinthians 1:3–11; James 1:2–4; 1 Peter 1:3–7; 4:12–19

WEEK 3

BETWEEN YOU AND GOD

If your hand causes you to sin, cut it off. It is better for you to enter life maimed than with two hands to go into hell, where the fire never goes out. And if your foot causes you to sin, cut it off. It is better for you to enter life crippled than to have two feet and be thrown into hell. And if your eye causes you to sin, pluck it out. It is better for you to enter the kingdom of God with one eye than to have two eyes and be thrown into hell.

MARK 9:43−47

In some parts of Iran today, crime busting is serious business. Convicted thieves don't just go to jail. They get a finger cut off. If you don't want to spend the rest of your life counting with your toes, you learn to keep your hands off other people's property.

In the verses above, Jesus is not teaching Iran-like self-mutilation, because even a blind man can lust. Rather, he uses hyperbole, an exaggerated figure of speech, to emphasize the need for no-holds-barred action. The Bible clearly states: The wages of sin are death. And so he gives fair warning that if anything stands between you and God, you'd better get rid of it pronto, because otherwise you could spend the rest of eternity in the hothouse.

In the gospels, the story is told of a rich young man who approached Christ with the question: "What must I do to inherit eternal life?" (Mark 10:17). Jesus began reeling off the ten commandments, but the man interrupted and said he'd kept the commandments since he was a child. "One thing you lack," Christ replied. "Go, sell everything you have ... then come, follow me." The man's face fell. His bank account stood between him and salvation.

With Pontius Pilate, pride stood in the way. He had the unique opportunity to pardon Christ, but the crowd bellowed for crucifixion. Like many politicians in the public eye, Pilate didn't want people thinking he was a wimp. So he allowed Christ to be killed to spare his own reputation.

Any number of things can stand between you and God. It may be a love relationship, a six-pack of Bud, a flashy car. Perhaps it's ambition, your bedroom mirror, a carton of Marlboro Lights. Maybe it's a hot temper, a ravenous appetite, a lustful thought.

Whatever it is, get rid of it. For God's sake, amputate. Yes, *for God's sake*. Heaven can't wait.

See also: Romans 6:23; 7:14–25; Hebrews 12:1–3; 1 John 1:9

PASSING GRADE

Enter through the narrow gate. For wide is the gate and broad is the road that leads to destruction, and many enter through it. But small is the gate and narrow the road that leads to life, and only a few find it.

MATTHEW 7:13–14

Nestled amidst rolling green farmland in the northwestern corner of West Virginia, Parkersburg's Blennerhassett High was embroiled with controversy a few years ago. Not about gangs or drugs or sex or any of the usual things. The problem was that the earth science teacher gave Ds and Fs to sixty percent of his students, and the principal wanted him to inflate the grades, to be more "fair."

But the teacher, one of the district's best, wouldn't budge. He wasn't about to boost grades merely to get the principal and certain parents off his back. He comprehended what they didn't—students have to work fairly hard *not* to pass.

"One student didn't understand how he could go from a C to an F in three weeks," the teacher told one reporter. "Well, he didn't turn in his exercise book with all his class paperwork for the six-week period. That's a zero. That pulls the average down."

45

Other students wouldn't take their book home even if told they'd be tested the next day on specific pages. They'd score fourteen out of fifty points, and then ask why they were getting a D.

People's feelings about heaven and hell are, in some regards, similar to the Blennerhassett High controversy. They act as if God were Scrooge, handing out bushels of passes to Death Valley when he could just as easily distribute tickets to Tahiti. They suspect God of being unfair, of setting standards too high. After all, you can't just set the high-jump bar at ten feet and expect miracles.

God's standards are, of course, extremely high. But he's not looking for miracles, because heaven cannot be attained by heroics. In fact, it takes more effort for the wicked to reach hell than it does for the righteous to reach heaven. Credit Jesus for that. When it comes right down to it, Romans 6:23 says it best: "The wages of sin is death, but the gift of God is eternal life in Christ Jesus our Lord." In other words, you work your way to hell. Heaven is a handout, delivered by Jesus.

That's the good news. The bad news is that most people are too proud to accept it.

See also: Romans 3:20–28; Ephesians 2:8–10; Philippians 2:13

DEVILISH SCHEMES

Put on the full armor of God so that you can take your stand against the devil's schemes. For our struggle is not against flesh and blood, but against the rulers, against the authorities, against the powers of this dark world and against the spiritual forces of evil in the heavenly realms.

EPHESIANS 6:11–12

Many people grow up thinking of the devil as a Saturday morning cartoon character, dressed in red long johns, with a pair of threatening-but-cute horns protruding from his head. He's as scary as Mickey Mouse with a pitchfork, as frightening as a rubber snake. As might be expected, this Hanna-Barbera image resembles the real thing about as much as Yogi Bear resembles a marauding grizzly.

In his book *The Screwtape Letters*, C. S. Lewis creates fictional correspondence between a wise old devil, Screwtape, and his young protégé Wormwood. Screwtape's letters to the young apprentice help teach him the ropes, and at the same time, reveal a behind-the-scenes look at Satan's true character and schemes:

You will say that these are very small sins; and doubtless, like all young tempters, you are anxious to be able to report spectacular wickedness. But do remember, the only thing that matters is the extent to which you separate the man from the Enemy [God]. It does not matter how small the sins are, provided that their cumulative effect is to edge the man away from the Light and out into the Nothing. Murder is no better than cards if cards can do the trick. Indeed, the safest road to Hell is the gradual one—the gentle slope, soft underfoot, without sudden turnings, without milestones, without signposts.

If you take God seriously, you also ought to take Satan seriously. He's a cunning strategist, both ruthless and relentless. That's why the apostle Peter gives this strong warning in 1 Peter 5:8–9: "Keep a cool head. Stay alert. The Devil is poised to pounce, and would like nothing better than to catch you napping. Keep your guard up" (*The Message*).

Heed the warning. One reason Satan flourishes is that he's treated like a pussycat instead of a roaring lion. Beware of the disguise.

See also: Matthew 4:1–11; 2 Corinthians 11:14–15; James 4:7–8; 1 John 3:7–10

GOOD MORNING, AMERICA

My people come to you, as they usually do, and sit before you to listen to your words, but they do not put them into practice. With their mouths they express devotion, but their hearts are greedy for unjust gain. Indeed, to them you are nothing more than one who sings love songs with a beautiful voice and plays an instrument well, for they hear your words but do not put them into practice.

EZEKIEL 33:31–32

From one day to the next, the news doesn't change much. On a research trip to the library, I scanned newspaper articles from a few years ago. They might as well have been written today.

On that particular morning as America woke up, the early front-runner for the White House ended his campaign prematurely in the doghouse—amidst accusations that he'd gone "under cover" with somebody other than his wife ... The *Wall Street Journal* read like the *National Enquirer*, littered with reports that New York's brightest financial wizards were but pin-striped outlaws who traded inside tips to supplement their million-dollar incomes ... A leading recording artist was slapped with a $90 million lawsuit by a young woman who claimed he gave her genital herpes and then told her the disease was "God's way of giving your sex life a rest" ... A popular faith healer pleaded for several million dollars from his TV faithful lest God make good an alleged threat to "call me home" ... The Marines guarding our Moscow embassy faced spy charges after trading secrets for sex ... A defense contractor with $11 billion in annual sales billed the government $1,118.26 for the plastic cap on a stool leg ... The House and Senate Select Committees found that the president permitted overzealous aides to conduct illegal operations right under his nose ... A leading televangelist, who spent his $1.6 million annual salary

48

on such things as gold-plated bathroom faucets, Rolls Royce autos, chandelier-lit closets, and air-conditioned doghouses, fell on hard times after admitting he'd paid $265,000 in hush money to cover up an afternoon of adultery with a 21-year-old church secretary—a tryst arranged by another popular evangelist ... and on and on and onand onandonandon.

On that particular morning as America woke up, the womanizing presidential hopeful blamed the media for the mess he was in ... The president blasted the press for stirring up unnecessary news and refused to admit responsibility for the chaos around him ... The philandering and fast-living televangelist insisted his troubles were part of a "diabolical plot" by rival preachers ... and on and on andonandonandon.

On that particular morning as America woke up, and on *this* particular morning as you crawl out of bed, Satan was and *is* on the prowl—looking for those of us to whom ethical behavior does not become important until the roof caves in, searching for those of us to whom Christian principles and morality are maintained not as guideposts of conduct, but as props to make us look as if we were the good folks.

See also: Malachi 4:1–2; Matthew 25:31–46; Titus 1:16; James 2:14–17

TROUBLE IN THE FOREST

> *Each one should test his own actions. Then he can take pride in himself, without comparing himself to somebody else.*

> GALATIANS 6:4

Reprinted below is an article from the Springfield, Oregon, Public Schools newsletter. It's a parable that packs a big punch:

Once upon a time, the animals decided they should do something meaningful to meet the problems of the new world. So they organized a school.

They adopted an activity curriculum of running, climbing, swimming, and flying. To make it easier to administer the curriculum, all the animals took all the subjects.

The duck was excellent in swimming; in fact, better than his instructor. But he made only passing grades in flying, and was very poor in running. Since he was slow in running, he had to drop swimming and stay after school to practice running. This caused his webbed feet to be badly worn, so that he was only average in swimming. But average was quite acceptable, so nobody worried about that—except the duck.

The rabbit started at the top of his class in running, but developed a nervous twitch in his leg muscles because of so much make-up work in swimming.

The squirrel was excellent in climbing, but he encountered constant frustration in flying class because his teacher made him start from the ground up instead of from the treetop down. He developed "charley horses" from overexertion, and so only got a C in climbing and a D in running.

The eagle was a problem child and was severely disciplined for being a nonconformist. In climbing classes he beat all the others to the top of the tree, but insisted on using his own way to get there. . . .

The point of the story is obvious: God has given each of us a very special set of abilities and capabilities. They are ours alone. When we try to be like others, we're like a rabbit that tries to swim or a squirrel that tries to fly. It's frustrating and phony trying to be anybody but yourself. And it is not much fun. True satisfaction comes when you realize you are a unique creation of God—freckles, flat feet, bony knees, long nose, big ears, and all.

So stop comparing yourself to others. Just for today, enjoy being you!

See also: Romans 12:2–8; 1 Corinthians 12:12–26

WANNA BE'S

From him [Christ] the whole body, joined and held together by every supporting ligament, grows and builds itself up in love, as each part does its work.

EPHESIANS 4:16

All around are people who seem "better" than you. They get better grades, have better looks, drive better cars, work better jobs, tell better jokes. If only you had their clothes, their abilities, their brains, their boyfriend; if only you could switch lives and homes and friends and families. Wouldn't it be nice just to be *them?*

Yesterday you read a whimsical article about a bunch of frustrated animals. Their problems were simple enough: by trying so hard to be like others, they lost their own sense of identity. Their successes turned to failures; excellence degenerated to mediocrity. The incredible satisfaction that came from being a web-footed, hard-swimming duck was lost when the duck tried to race around the running track. In the same manner, the rabbit was a failure on the swim team. As a flyer, the squirrel simply proved the law of gravity was still intact. And the eagle was no more successful than a bowling ball as a climber.

If you're a duck, stick to water and thank God you have funny-looking feet. You'll be successful—as long as you paddle with all of your might and quit worrying about running and climbing. So what if you waddle when you walk? That's the way God made ducks.

If you're a rabbit, you'll experience burnout if you continually try to make it on the swim team.

And beware of challenging the territory of the eagle, for the eagle may decide it likes you better for breakfast than for competition.

In the end, you'll do much better (and the body of Christ will work more smoothly) if you concentrate exclusively on being *yourself* and allow others to be *themselves.* Don't try to be like those

51

around you, and don't expect them to be like you. Relax. Get comfortable with your own style, looks, and surroundings. Learn to enjoy your own, very special, very unique corner of the forest.

Most of all, realize that when God made you, he was pleased. He could do no better.

See also: Genesis 1:26–31; 2 Corinthians 10:12–18; Galatians 6:4

POINTS TO PONDER: IDENTITY

If anyone would come after me, he must deny himself and take up his cross and follow me. For whoever wants to save his life will lose it, but whoever loses his life for me will find it.

MATTHEW 16:24–25

When a man is all wrapped up in himself he makes a pretty small package.

JOHN RUSKIN

Man's problem rises from the fact that he has not only lost the way, but he has lost the address.

NICOLAS BERDYAEV

Jesus Christ never met an unimportant person. That is why God sent his Son to die for us. If someone dies for you, you must be important.

M. C. CLEVELAND

If you have anything really valuable to contribute to the world it will come through the expression of your own personality, that single spark of divinity that sets you off and makes you different from every other living creature.

BRUCE BARTON

Men are not against you; they are merely for themselves.

GENE FOWLER

Have confidence that if you have done a little thing well, you can do a bigger thing well, too.

STOREY

Here is Christian identity: I know my past, where I came from. I came from God. I know what went wrong. I tried to play God instead of being satisfied to be a real man. I know my future. My destiny is Christ. And I know the present. I can face myself now— my problems, my hang-ups, my assets, my faults—because I have turned myself over to God.

LEIGHTON FORD

The world is a looking glass and gives back to every man the reflection of his own face.

WILLIAM MAKEPEACE THACKERAY

He who knows himself best esteems himself least.

H. G. BOHN

Do not attempt to do a thing unless you are sure of yourself; but do not relinquish it simply because someone else is not sure of you.

STEWART E. WHITE

The greatest burden we have to carry in life is self; the most difficult thing we have to manage is self.

HANNAH WHITALL SMITH

Modern youth alternates between abysmal hang-ups and fanatical commitments. Psychologists call their malady an "identity crisis." Its chief symptom is the cry: "Who am I?" To them I say, "Have a confrontation with yourself. Then have a confrontation with Jesus Christ."

BILLY GRAHAM

Either heaven or hell will have continuous background music piped in. Which one you think it is tells a lot about your personality.

BILL VAUGHAN

Everybody thinks of changing humanity and nobody thinks of changing himself.

LEO TOLSTOY

He who falls in love with himself will have no rivals.

BENJAMIN FRANKLIN

You can always tell when a man is a great way from God: when he is always talking about himself, how good he is.

DWIGHT L. MOODY

Many could forego heavy meals, a full wardrobe, a fine house; it is the ego that they cannot forego.

MOHANDAS K. GANDHI

See also: John 12:43; Romans 2:7–8; 5:7–8; Philippians 2:1–8

WEEK 4

HANGING TOUGH

Is any one of you in trouble? He should pray.

JAMES 5:13

Some days are tougher than others. You wake up late, with only ten minutes before you must be out the front door. You race for the bathroom, only to find your kid sister hogging it for keeps. You jerk on the handle, which pulls off in your hand.

At school, your history teacher adorns the top of your midterm with a big red F, your boyfriend is flirting with the new girl from Minnesota, and you forget your locker combination. And then at lunch, you spill a carton of yogurt in your lap. You want to scream, but when you accidentally bite your tongue you start to cry instead.

On days like this, I recall the story of the four guys who decided to go mountain climbing one weekend. Approaching the peak, one of the climbers slipped over a cliff, tumbled about sixty feet, and crash-landed on a small ledge.

"Bob, are you okay?" his three friends shouted from above.

"I'm alive . . . but I think I busted both my arms!" a weak voice responded.

"Well, hang in there," yelled his friends. "We'll toss a rope down and pull you up. Just lie still!"

"Fine," answered Bob.

Shortly after lowering one end of the rope, they started tugging and grunting together, working feverishly to pull their wounded companion to safety. When they had him about three-fourths of the way up, they suddenly remembered he said he'd broken *both* of his arms.

"Bob! If you broke both your arms, how in the world are you hanging on?"

"With my TEEEEEEEEEEEEETH . . ."

On days when all you can do is hold on by your teeth, not even friends are company. Chances are, they're bringing bad news

56

anyway. Remember Job and his friends? They had all kinds of inane advice on how he could improve things.

In times of trouble, you need to avoid bum advice from well-meaning people. You need to act quickly and decisively. There's no time for Plan B. Your lifeline is Jesus Christ. Grab on tight. And then pray like crazy, if only through your teeth.

See also: Proverbs 19:23; John 16:33; Romans 8:38–39; Hebrews 12:2–3

YES OR NO

Simply let your "Yes" be "Yes," and your "No," "No."

MATTHEW 5:37

At the heart of life's every decision, even the most difficult ones, are some fairly simple yes-or-no questions. Each situation we encounter, every alternative we face, can be reduced to either a *yes* or a *no.*

Should I get up when the alarm rings? Should I go to school? Should I eat breakfast? Should I talk to my dad? Should I light up in the rest room? Should I kick the habit once and for all? Should I go to the party? Should I have a beer? *Yes* or *no?*

Throughout the day we make thousands of such decisions. Should I ask Becky out? Should I stay home and save my money? Should I order an all-you-can-eat platter of shrimp? Should I stick to my diet? Should I wear black shoes? Should I get married next year? Should I wait? *Yes* or *no?*

The necessity of making yes-or-no decisions is inescapable. All of the great historical decisions have been made, in the end, by a simple *yes* or *no* response. Should the colonies fight Mother England for their independence? Should the North declare war on the

South? Should the United States respond to Japan's sneak attack? Should we drop The Bomb?

The most important decision you will ever have to make in your life—the one that determines your destiny for all of eternity—also comes down to *yes* or *no*. Do you believe Jesus is the Christ, the Son of God? Do you think he was just some nut with delusions of grandeur? Do you believe he died for you on the cross? Was he just an ideologue in a bathrobe and sandals who was killed for stirring up controversy? Do you believe he loves you? Well, do you? Answer the question: *Yes* or *no?*

Eternal life is a simple decision. But it's so important that the angels of heaven have their ears cocked to hear your response. What will it be? Just say *yes* or *no*.

See also: Joshua 24:15; Luke 15:8–10

MY FAVORITE WORD

This day I call heaven and earth as witnesses against you that I have set before you life and death, blessings and curses. Now choose life, so that you and your children may live and that you may love the Lord your God, listen to his voice, and hold fast to him.

DEUTERONOMY 30:19–20

Of all the words in the English language, my favorite is *yes*. What other word makes people more happy or offers more hope? What other word can bring a bigger or faster smile?

"Yes, the exam's been canceled."

"Yes, the X-rays are clear."

"Yes, you're hired."

"Yes, I will marry you."

Yes brings the good news. It seals the commitment. It gets rockets launched and new cars designed and shopping malls built. *Yes* is affirmation that you're on the right track, that you're doing a good job. If I knew I were going deaf and could choose the last word I'd ever hear, that word would be *yes*.

Yes is at least as old as the words of Moses in Deuteronomy: "This day ... I have set before you life and death, blessings and curses. Now choose life."

The first day of the rest of your life began when you said *yes* to God. That may have happened ten years ago; it may have occurred yesterday. On that day, whenever it was, you "chose life." Eternal life.

Pause a few minutes right now. Think back to that special day and to the events leading to your decision. As you recollect, jot down a few of the details that come to mind. In addition, make note of any changes in your life that you've noticed since then.

I became a Christian on or about _____

because I felt _____,

and because I needed _____.

Since becoming a Christian, I've noticed several changes, including _____.

Now, are there areas of your life that still need work? Think about things you've held back from God, attitudes that keep him at arm's length. What decisions have you made where you've said no to him, whether consciously or unconsciously? Work this week at turning a no into a yes.

It's only a word, but it makes all the difference in the world.

See also: Matthew 9:28; John 11:27; 21:16; 2 Corinthians 1:19–20; Revelation 22:20

JUST SAY NO

So I find this law at work: When I want to do good, evil is right there with me. For in my inner being I delight in God's law; but I see another law at work in the members of my body, waging war against the law of my mind and making me a prisoner of the law of sin at work within my members. What a wretched man I am! Who will rescue me from this body of death? Thanks be to God—through Jesus Christ our Lord!

ROMANS 7:21–25

As you read yesterday, the word *yes* is full of optimism and hope. It signals new life and causes smiles to blossom. It may be everybody's favorite word, but beware.

Though *yes* brings happiness, it also brings much heartache. In fact, *yes* can get you in more trouble than you ever thought possible. The wisdom of the hour is, "Just say *no*."

There are times when *no* is the absolute best, most positive response you can make:

"My parents are going away for the weekend. How about spending the night?"

Just say *no*. Virtue is too precious to lose in one night.

"Hey dude, got me some good dope. Wanna get blitzed Friday night?"

Just say *no*. "Good dope" is a contradiction in terms.

"What's your problem? Everybody's doing it. Say *yes* and quit worrying."

Just say *no*. Your worries will start if you say *yes*.

Unfortunately, it's not often easy to say *no*. Take a few minutes right now, and think about those times you said *yes* when you know you should have said *no*. Wrong decisions can keep you awake all night. They can haunt you for months and may even impact the rest of your life.

If you went to bed last night with a weight of guilt on your shoulders, you can be out from under the burden by bedtime tonight. When you're at the end of your rope, who will rescue you? Is there anyone who can do anything to help? Isn't that the real question?

As the apostle Paul said in the verse above (with a slightly different emphasis provided from another version of the Bible): "The answer, thank God, is that Jesus Christ can and does" (*The Message*). He acted to set things right, to make sense of this life of contradictions, to pull you back from the influence of sin.

It is Jesus Christ, and *only* Jesus Christ, who gives you the power to say no, and to serve God with all your heart and mind.

See also: 2 Corinthians 2:14–15; 2 Timothy 2:22

SLIP SLIDING AWAY

Each one is tempted when, by his own evil desire, he is dragged away and enticed. Then, after desire has conceived, it gives birth to sin; and sin, when it is full-grown, gives birth to death.

JAMES 1:14–15

A lot of hormones were flying whenever Danny and Dawn were together. Both were Christians and both thought they could control their relationship. But they were far past the holding hands and kissing stage, and even when they sat in a crowded cafeteria they couldn't seem to get close enough to each other.

The harder they tried to keep things under control, the more frustrated they both became. Before long, their relationship with Christ was on the rocks. And this wonderful couple that everybody thought would last forever was breaking apart—fast. Finally, they called it quits as a couple to salvage their love for God before it was too late.

However, Danny couldn't stay away from the phone. *No big deal*, he thought, *it's just a phone call.*

Dawn was thrilled to hear his familiar voice on the line, and when he asked her out, she was quick to say yes. *There's nothing wrong with just seeing him*, she reasoned.

After the movie, the night was still young. So Danny drove around for a little while, feeling comfort in Dawn's presence beside him. *So far, so good*, he said to himself. *So what if we get home just a little late?*

When Danny eventually pulled off the road and parked beneath a stand of trees, they both had an uneasy feeling. They'd been down this same path before, and knew exactly where it led: straight to the backseat.

Nearly two hours later when they pulled back onto the road, neither said a word. They were both deep in thought, trying to recollect how an innocent evening together could end in the same old way in the same old place, with both feeling so empty and so desperately guilty.

It was a sad, quiet thought that haunted them for nine long months—right up until the birth of their unexpected baby.

See also: Proverbs 26:27; 1 Thessalonians 4:3–8

TOUGH DECISIONS

> *Love the Lord your God with all your heart and with all your soul and with all your strength.*
>
> DEUTERONOMY 6:5

Making decisions has never been particularly easy for me. Girls whom I dated wanted me to be more decisive. I drove them crazy because I had no idea what I wanted to do when I asked them out. I just wanted to be together. Where we ended up wasn't important to me.

"Well, what do you want to do?" I'd ask once we were in the car.

If it was a new relationship, the girl would generally shrug and smile. "Whatever you want."

I'd smile right back. "I don't really care. Where would *you* like to go?"

"It doesn't matter. *You* decide."

We'd go back and forth like that, as if playing verbal ping-pong. Only after an extended volley would we settle on a movie or restaurant or some other place where we could spend the evening and all of my money. And then I would promptly get lost trying to get there.

Perhaps that's why it was so tough when I had to decide what I was going to do about Jesus Christ. I couldn't just ignore him. His claims and promises were too insistent. But I knew that if I followed in his footsteps, if I said yes to him, I must *comparatively* say no to everything else. I had to *comparatively* relinquish my devotion to my desires and dreams, to my family, and even to my own life. I knew God demanded my complete devotion. Not a part. Not even the biggest part. But all of it.

That's the way it is with Christ. If we love him with all our heart and with all our soul and with all our strength, there's really no room for competing loves. If we follow Moses' advice to the Israelites and love God with our full emotional, mental, and physical capabilities, all other loves and desires pale by comparison. If he is truly Lord, his throne cannot be shared.

A tough decision? Yes. We must necessarily forsake all other loves. It's certainly not an easy decision. But it's a decision he demands we make. And like it or not, we must make it daily.

See also: 1 Samuel 12:24; Psalm 1; Mark 8:34–38; Luke 14:26

POINTS TO PONDER: CHOICE

Choose for yourselves this day whom you will serve.... But as for me and my household, we will serve the Lord.

JOSHUA 24:15

God has no need of marionettes. He pays men the compliment of allowing them to live without him if they choose. But if they live without him in this life, they must also live without him in the next.

LEON MORRIS

I hate to see things done by halves. If it be right, do it boldly; if it be wrong leave it undone.

BERNARD BILPIN

God's love shouts for our salvation; Satan's enticements whisper for our damnation. The one is like a bullhorn; the other as light as a tickle. We must decide which voice we hear, and at what volume. The choice is wholly ours to make; our destiny, solely ours to determine. If the choice is not consciously taken, the choice has nonetheless been unconsciously made.

S. RICKLY CHRISTIAN

Between two evils, choose neither; between two goods, choose both.

TRYON EDWARDS

It is possible for a man to run against the wrong object and bend his lance for good.

A. W. TOZER

Father, make of me a crisis man. Bring those I contact to decision. Let me not be a milepost on a single road; make me a fork, that men must turn one way or another on facing Christ in me.

JIM ELLIOT

When a Christian is in the wrong place, his right place is empty.

T. J. BACH

As sure as I lived, I knew that I possessed a will, and that when I willed to do something or willed not to do something, nobody else was making the decision.

AUGUSTINE OF HIPPO

Perhaps no mightier conflict of mind occurs ever again in a life-time than that first decision to unseat one's own tooth.

GENE FOWLER

To be a Christian, or not to be, is not a matter of being a somewhat better man, or a man perhaps not quite so good. It is a matter of life or death.

JAMES DENNEY

He who chooses the beginning of a road chooses the place it leads to. It is the means that determine the end.

HARRY EMERSON FOSDICK

A man is too apt to forget that in this world he cannot have every-thing. A choice is all that is left him.

H. MATTHEWS

In darkness there is no choice. It is light that enables us to see the differences between things; and it is Christ who gives us light.

A. W. HARE

Let it be known on whose side you are. If there is any doubt about it, something is wrong.

ANONYMOUS

We make our decisions, and then our decisions turn around and make us.

F. W. BOREHAM

The block of granite which was an obstacle in the pathway of the weak becomes a stepping-stone in the pathway of the strong.

THOMAS CARLYLE

Once I make up my mind, I'm full of indecision.

OSCAR LEVANT

See also: Deuteronomy 30:19–20; Proverbs 1:28–29; 2 Corinthians 5:17; Revelation 3:15–16

WEEK 5

SERIOUS TROUBLE

I am convinced that neither death nor life, neither angels nor demons, neither the present nor the future, nor any powers, neither height nor depth, nor anything else in all creation, will be able to separate us from the love of God that is in Christ Jesus our Lord.

ROMANS 8:38–39

Some days you feel like you should have stayed in bed. Things start out bad and progressively get worse. If you've got it bad today, consider the plight of this young construction worker as detailed on his company's accident form:

When I got to the building, I found that the hurricane had knocked off some bricks around the top. So I rigged up a beam with a pulley at the top of the building and hoisted up a couple barrels full of bricks.

When I had fixed the damaged area, there were a lot of bricks left over. Then I went to the bottom and began releasing the line. Unfortunately, the barrel of bricks was much heavier than I was—and before I knew what was happening, the barrel started coming down, jerking me up.

I decided to hang on since I was too far off the ground by then to jump, and halfway up I met the barrel of bricks coming down fast. I received a hard blow on my shoulder. I then continued to the top, banging my head against the beam, and getting my fingers pinched and jammed in the pulley. When the barrel hit the ground hard, it burst its bottom, allowing the bricks to spill out.

I was now heavier than the barrel. So I started down again at high speed. Halfway down I met the barrel coming up fast, and received severe injuries to my shins. When I hit the ground, I landed on the pile of spilled bricks, getting several painful cuts and deep bruises.

At this point, I must have lost my presence of mind because I let go of my grip on the line. The barrel came down fast—giving me another blow on my head and putting me in the hospital.

I respectfully request sick leave.

When you've got it *that* bad, you need help. You don't want somebody to say, "Cheer up." You want somebody to be with you, to share your pain. You want somebody who understands; not somebody who just got off the turnip truck or crawled out of the ivory tower. Experience helps. If somebody has known pain personally, chances are good they can help alleviate yours. You want somebody who won't run when the going gets tough, somebody who will never leave you or forsake you ...

That "somebody" sounds an awful lot like Jesus.

See also: Proverbs 19:23; John 16:33; Hebrews 12:2–3

WOODLAND HILLS TRAGEDY

You shall not murder.

EXODUS 20:13

A few years ago, workmen repossessed a boxcar-sized dumpster from the yard of Malvin R. Weisberg of Woodland Hills, California. When the padlocked doors were opened, workers faced a wall of wet boxes and a stench that was as thick as fog.

As the cartons were unloaded, the bottom of one suddenly tore, and clear plastic containers tumbled to the floor. Out of one pint-sized tub spilled something wrapped in cotton gauze. When the workers gathered around to examine the contents, they were horrified. Several threw up on the spot.

"It was human flesh, pure and simple," said the yard supervisor. "What I saw was two hands, two feet, and a mutilated body."

Eventually, 16,433 bodies were retrieved from the storage container—the smaller ones in cottage cheese tubs, the larger in gallon buckets. Each was a baby who died before birth. The cause of death: abortion.

The real tragedy is not that one man collected nearly 17,000 dead babies in his backyard over a four-year period. The real tragedy is that there are that many children aborted nationwide every three to four days. In the next twelve months, nearly 1.5 million unborn babies will lose their lives in the United States; millions more in other countries. To compound the tragedy, millions of adoption requests will remain unmet because there aren't enough babies to go around.

Some people believe we should look the other way when it comes to abortion, if only because of civil rights. It's a free country, and nobody's supposed to have the right to impose religious beliefs on another person. That's true, but we also live in a country wherein nobody is granted the right to deprive another person of life and liberty. To do so is not imposing a religious belief, but violating a principle that's basic to every culture in the world: Thou shalt not kill.

Nevertheless, the killing continues. It doesn't make the newspapers because abortion is a quiet death. But someday . . . someday, the tragedy and injustice of this silent holocaust will be as obvious as is our hindsight today of slavery or the mass exterminations in Nazi Germany.

See also: Deuteronomy 30:19; Psalm 139:13–16; Matthew 19:14

A LANGUAGE BARRIER

Who is wise and understanding among you? Let him show it by his good life, by deeds done in the humility that comes from wisdom.

JAMES 3:13

When I graduated a few years ago with a communications degree from Stanford, I considered myself fluent in English. Upon graduation, I was hired as an obituary writer.

Among my first newspaper stories: *Joe McGee, 81, died yesterday after being gored by a runaway forklift. An area native, he was a member of the Forklift Operators Society of America and the Plentiful Harvest Baptist Church. McGee is survived by his mother, Ella Mae, 102.* Three sentences; each short and understandable.

I still do okay with the language, but I understand less and less. If you ask me, most politicians and economists don't speak English. Astronomers, with their talk of anagalactic goings-on, are just as bad. And I was left scratching my head when I read a movie review the other day. The film was criticized because its "dim-witted sanctity begs to be beaten into lean meat." I'd much rather somebody just say the movie was a dog.

I wish Christians spoke more plainly as well. Too many times we shield our experiences and feelings in a kind of Christian lingo. I ooze pity for the uninitiated when they are "witnessed to" about being "born again." Huh? It sounds like some court case involving a strange birthing procedure. Talk about "being saved by the blood" sounds like the plot of the next Stephen King thriller, while "soul winning" could be a new release from Motown Records.

Such talk may sound rather spiritual. But *sounding* spiritual has never been the same as *being* spiritual. That's what Christ found with the Pharisees. These religious honchos talked godly and prayed loudly. But they lived pretty godless lives, and their prayers just bounced off the wall.

In the end, actions speak louder than words. They always have and they always will. You might consider that the next time you *tell* somebody you're a Christian. Try *showing* them as well.

See also: James 1:26; 1 Peter 3:1–2

FISHLESS FISHERMEN

*"Come, follow me," Jesus said, "and I will make
you fishers of men."*

MATTHEW 4:19

A few people I know became Christians just by reading the
Bible. But the vast majority, myself included, would never have
established a personal relationship with Jesus Christ unless somebody first talked to them about his love, his forgiveness, his death
and resurrection. With that in mind, I pass along the following parable by John M. Drescher:

*Now it came to pass that a group existed who called them-
selves fishermen. And lo, there were many fish in the waters all
around. Week after week, those who called themselves fishermen met
and talked about the abundance of fish, and searched for better methods of fishing.*

*They loved slogans such as "Every fisherman is a fisher,"
sponsored special "Fishermen's Campaigns," convened nationwide
congresses to promote fishing, constructed beautiful "Fishing Head-
quarters," and built large printing houses to publish fishing guides.
One thing they didn't do, however. They didn't fish.*

*In addition to meeting regularly, they organized a board of
those with great vision to send fishermen to faraway streams and
lakes. The board, in turn, hired staffs and appointed committees, but
they did not fish.*

*Expensive training centers were built to teach fishermen how
to fish, the nature of fish, and where to fish. Those who taught had
doctorates in fishology, but they did not fish. Many were graduated,
given fishing licenses, and sent to do full-time fishing. But they spent
their time building power plants to pump water for fish, plowing new*

waterways, supplying fishing equipment, and visiting fish hatcheries. They didn't fish.

One day after a stirring meeting on "The Necessity of Fishing," one young fellow actually went fishing. The next day he reported he had caught two outstanding fish. He was honored for his excellent catch, and scheduled to speak everywhere. To have the time for that, he had to quit fishing.

Now it's true that many fishermen sacrificed and put up with many difficulties. Some lived near the water and bore the smell of fish every day. They were ridiculed about their fishermen's clubs. So imagine how hurt some were when one day a person suggested they were really not fishermen. It made them stop and think.

But after all, are you really a fisherman if year after year you never fish?

See also: Isaiah 6:5–8; James 1:22–25

■■
■

SHOW OR TELL

Dear friends, I urge you, as aliens and strangers in the world, to abstain from sinful desires, which war against your soul. Live such good lives among the pagans that, though they accuse you of doing wrong, they may see your good deeds and glorify God on the day he visits us.

1 PETER 2:11–12

When Christ talked about God to everyday people he met on the street, he tried to be as understandable as possible. He used a lot of parables, or word pictures, and told many stories. But he knew it took more than words to communicate. It took action. He didn't just *tell* people about God's love, he *showed* them love.

What would you do if you woke up mute one morning—you couldn't say a word? What if others could discover Jesus based only on your actions, instead of your words? Take a few minutes to jot down a few ideas below about how you might visibly display Jesus in various areas of your life.

At school, my friends would be able to see Jesus in my life if I would: _____.

At home, my family would be able to see Jesus in my life if I would: _____.

At work, my boss and fellow employees would be able to see Jesus in my life if I would: _____.

See also: James 2:14–26

█

LOOK WHO'S TALKING

No one lights a lamp and puts it in a place where it will be hidden, or under a bowl. Instead he puts it on its stand, so that those who come in may see the light.

LUKE 11:33

When I first became a Christian, I got a rash just thinking about talking to somebody else about God. It was worse than the mental gymnastics I'd go through before calling a girl for the first time. When the topic of God came up, I developed a sudden shy attack. My mind turned to Jell-O and my mouth felt like a sweater.

At the heart of these feelings was my desire not to offend people. My friendships were important to me, as was my reputation. And so, not wanting others to think of me as a shallow-minded religious weirdo, I mostly kept quiet about my faith. Witnessing became nothing more than smiling a lot, occasionally inviting somebody to church, being nice, and hoping others would somehow "catch on."

But it wasn't long before I noticed an amazing thing happening: *nothing.* Nobody caught on to anything. Though I saw the needs and emptiness in my non-Christian friends, I was paralyzed to help. The reason was simple. I cared more about how *they* saw me than how God saw me.

About that time, I discussed my feelings with an older Christian whom I respected. He wasn't exactly gushy about his faith, but he'd look you in the eye when he talked about Jesus. And he'd tell you openly that his prime goal in life was to take as many people with him into heaven as possible. I've never forgotten his words to me.

"Rick, your life will never save anyone," he said. "Being a nice guy is fine, but people aren't won to God because of nice guys. They're won to God because of Jesus' life and death. And how will anybody know about Jesus' life and death unless you tell them?"

My feelings about evangelism didn't change overnight. In fact, my mouth sometimes still feels like a sweater when I talk to others about Jesus. But at least now I'm talking. When it comes to being the "light of the world," I may not be as powerful as a lightning bolt. Some days I feel no brighter than a lightning bug.

But as the saying goes, it only takes a spark to get a fire going.

See also: Matthew 5:13–16; John 1:6–9; 8:12

POINTS TO PONDER: EVANGELISM

Then Jesus came to them and said, "All authority in heaven and on earth has been given to me. Therefore go and make disciples of all nations, baptizing them in the name of the Father and of the Son and of the Holy Spirit, and teaching them to obey everything I have commanded you."

MATTHEW 28:18–20

Evangelism applies a supernatural remedy for the need of the world.

FARIS WHITESELL

75

Lighthouses don't fire guns or ring bells to call attention to their light; they just shine.

ANONYMOUS

Striving to win souls without earnest prayer, dogged love, and roll-up-your-sleeves effort is like trying to harvest corn on Sunset Beach. You don't reap where seeds have not been sown. Even with these things, it's hard work, because you're wrestling with the devil.

S. RICKLY CHRISTIAN

Christian: One who believes that the New Testament is a divinely inspired book admirably suited to the spiritual needs of his neighbors.

AMBROSE BIERCE

The real witnessing Christian does not talk about people he has "converted." Witnessing is hard work unless it is done in the Spirit, and then we can't brag about it.

WILLIAM R. BRIGHT

If a man has a soul—and he has—and if that soul can be won or lost for eternity—and it can—then the most important thing in the world is to bring that man to Jesus Christ.

ANONYMOUS

When a Christian is winning souls, he isn't messing around with sin.

GEORGE L. SMITH

Christianity is the land of beginning again.

W. A. CRISWELL

The trouble with some of us is that we have been inoculated with small doses of Christianity which keep us from catching the real thing.

LESLIE DIXON WEATHERHEAD

Love, truly cultivated, can breed new life.

S. RICKLY CHRISTIAN

Our business is to get people to close with Christ. Again and again they come up to the point of decision, but we don't push them over—we hardly try. We work their minds into thorough agreement that this and that must be done, but we don't clinch things on the spot. And so the metal cools again and nothing happens.

ARTHUR JOHN GOSSIP

Evangelism as the New Testament describes it is not child's play. Evangelism is work, often hard work. Yet it is not drudgery. It puts a person in good humor, and makes him truly human.

OSWALD C. J. HOFFMANN

When you need God, religion won't do.

S. RICKLY CHRISTIAN

Evangelism is the proclamation of the Gospel of the crucified and risen Christ, the only Redeemer of men, according to the Scriptures, with the purpose of persuading condemned and lost sinners to put their trust in God by receiving and accepting Christ as Savior through the power of the Holy Spirit, and to serve Christ as Lord in every calling of life and in the fellowship of his church, looking toward the day of his coming in glory.

WORLD CONGRESS ON EVANGELISM, BERLIN, 1966

Evangelism is a sharing of gladness.

ANONYMOUS

Something must really change in the world, and this can come only through men who themselves are changed. But when a man is changed under the influence of grace, then not only the state of his soul, but also his whole comportment, is changed. He is suddenly free from the old habits which kept him imprisoned, free from the rancor and remorse that consumed him. [He has] become whole in a broken world.

PAUL TOURNIER

When it comes to loving the unlovable, easy *doesn't* do it.

S. RICKLY CHRISTIAN

My feeling about people in whose conversion I have been allowed to play a part is always mixed with awe and even fear: such as a boy might feel on first being allowed to fire a rifle. The disproportion between his puny finger on the trigger and the thunder and lightning which follow is alarming.

C. S. LEWIS

See also: John 1:12–13; 3:1–21; Romans 3:23; 6:23

WEEK

6

LIFE ON THE HILL

Whoever is kind to the needy honors God.

PROVERBS 14:31

Most of us take our fast lives and fast food for granted. We seldom take a break from our stereos, schedules, and Big Macs to think about how much we really have ... or, for that matter, how much the rest of the world does *not* have. That's because "the world," with its billions of people and problems, seems too big and far away to really worry about.

As suggested by World Vision, a Christian world-relief agency, maybe we'd all be better off to think smaller. That is, we could imagine our planet of people represented by a small town of one thousand.

In our community, 180 of us live high on a hill, called the developed world, overlooking everything else. The other 820 live on the rocky bottom land, called the rest of the world. The fortunate 180 have more than 80 percent of the wealth of the town and more than half of all rooms, with two rooms per person. The 820 people down below have less than half of all the rooms, with five persons to a room.

According to the best estimates, those of us on the hill have 85 percent of all automobiles; 80 percent of all TV sets; 93 percent of all the telephones; and an average income per person of $5,000 per year. The rest of the town gets by on an average of about $700 per person, though many exist on $200 or less.

How does the fortunate group on the hill use its incredible wealth? As a group, these people spend less than one percent of their wealth to aid the bottom land. In the United States, for example, of every $100 earned $18.03 goes for food; $6.60 is spent on recreation and amusement; $5.80 is used for clothes; $2.40 is paid for alcohol; $1.50 buys tobacco; $1.30 is given for religious and charitable uses, and only a very small fraction of that goes to share the hill peoples' knowledge of Jesus Christ with the rest of the town.

Meanwhile, the town is unable to house, clothe, or feed 350 of its residents, 125 never get enough to eat, and 250 of the townspeople eat the wrong kinds of food. They have something called malnutrition, but they don't know it.

Jesus offered us a model and challenge when he instructed his followers to feed the hungry, give water to the thirsty, house strangers, clothe the naked, aid the sick, and visit the imprisoned. You see, as far as Christ is concerned there's no distinction between the hill people and the flatlanders.

He keeps hoping the people with the view will realize that. But many of them appear to spend a good part of their waking hours *asleep*—another luxury not shared by the rest of the town.

See also: Matthew 25:31–46; Hebrews 13:1–2; James 2:14–17

MISSING PART

Jesus said, "Let the little children come to me, and do not hinder them, for the kingdom of heaven belongs to such as these."

MATTHEW 19:14

By the time Lori was eighteen, she'd already had two children and was pregnant with a third. Under pressure from all sides to "put an end to this pregnancy nonsense," Lori consented to an abortion. At the time, her baby was twelve weeks old.

"The nurse assured me I'd feel no pain and that everything would be fine the next day," Lori told me in the course of research I was doing. "But the doctor dilated me with a series of metal rods that ripped up my cervix. I kept screaming and grabbing my tummy every time he scraped the suction tool around inside, but the nurse pinned me down, and the doctor told me to quit being so hysterical about something that was just a 'blob of jelly.' As if to prove his point, he kept smearing bloody bits of the child and placenta on the sheet beside me. 'See, there is no baby,' he said. 'Of course not,' I yelled. 'You just ground it to hamburger before my eyes!'"

After the abortion, Lori hemorrhaged terribly and had constant cramps. Finally, two weeks after the abortion, she went into labor. The contractions were horrible. "I staggered into the bathroom, and there I delivered a part of my baby the doctor had missed," she told me. "It was only about the size of a quarter, but there was no mistaking what it was. It was the head of my baby."

The horror of holding her child's head in her hands, coupled with incredible guilt, brought Lori to the verge of suicide. But in her darkest moment, she remembered the stories she'd heard as a child about God's forgiveness. And in the quietness of her room, she prayed for God to come into her heart and forgive her. But forgiveness was one thing; forgetting, something entirely different.

"Sometimes I still set the dinner table for three children instead of two," Lori said. "And I still have nightmares in which I am forced to watch my baby being ripped apart in front of me. But the most difficult aspect is that I simply miss my baby. I often wake up wanting to nurse my child, to hold my child. The doctor never told me I'd experience any of this. He said the only feeling I'd have would be relief. But I call it emptiness."

See also: 2 Chronicles 7:14; Psalm 139:13–16; Matthew 11:28

LIFE SENTENCE

Do not be misled: "Bad company corrupts good character." Come back to your senses as you ought, and stop sinning; for there are some who are ignorant of God—I say this to your shame.

1 CORINTHIANS 15:33–34

"Welcome to the State Penitentiary." The sign attempted a warm greeting. From a tower, a guard armed with a high-powered rifle watched as my friend stopped and took one final look at the door of the prison. With two life sentences, he had every reason to expect he'd never be free again.

At one point, my friend's future had been star bright. Though not the world's best student, he was a hometown athletic legend. The boy could *play*. His senior year in high school, he captained the basketball, baseball, and football teams. College scholarship offers rolled in, and scouts courted him at school.

But the future always seemed far away and my friend was attracted to the present. *Now* was all that mattered. He started running with a fast crowd, passing time with alcohol and colored pills. After one particular blur of parties which lasted an entire week, he drove two buddies to the home of some girls. He waited in the car. Minutes later they sprinted back shouting, "Drive! Drive! We shot a man!"

The scare sobered my friend and he broke off his relationship with the two others. But a year later, FBI detectives burst through his door and arrested him. Scared for their own futures, the pair fingered my friend for the crime. Justice was fickle and he was convicted of the murder.

"Ordinary people can sometimes get into extraordinary trouble," he says now, looking back on the incident. Their lives don't end up the way they're "supposed to." Little wrongs lead to bigger wrongs, and soon they're in over their head.

Maybe you know the feeling. Perhaps, like my friend, you've made some wrong choices along the way. Maybe time has gotten away from you, and you find yourself slip-sliding away—away from where you know God wants you to be. Perhaps you know what it's like to lie awake at 3 A.M. because of overwhelming guilt or to cry yourself to sleep night after night because of some past sin.

Thankfully, wrong choices, actions, and thoughts are forgivable. Kneeling in his roach-infested cell, my friend eventually found the transforming power and love of Jesus Christ. And years later, he received a full parole and pardon.

Though the closest brush most people have with the law is to spot a flashing red light in their rearview mirror, they can still be walled in by a prison of sin. If you're in that position, Jesus Christ can open the door and give you a full pardon. As the psalmist says, "The Lord sets prisoners free." That includes you and me, too.

See also: Psalm 51:1–12; Isaiah 1:18; Romans 6:23

EXTRAVAGANT TIME

I awoke and looked around. My sleep had been pleasant to me.

JEREMIAH 31:26

You push the little button down—a simple effort that guarantees your alarm will not ring. With no obnoxious buzz to jolt you awake, a dreamlike smile sweeps your mind and you stretch once, twice. Feeling like an heir to some latter-day throne, you pull your blanket up over your shoulders and doze off into never-never land . . .

Turning off an alarm is an extravagant pleasure—on par with walking barefoot in the mud. Actions like these keep the cobwebs out. Without them, we close our eyes at seventeen and open them at sixty-five.

So loosen up today. If you need some ideas on how to go about it, lavish yourself with some of the following:

Smile at a child. Smile at the child's parents, too. Tell them they've got a good-looking kid—even if he looks like a lizard. Or round up a couple of friends, dig out a jump rope, and have an old-fashioned aerobic workout. If you want to make a friend for life, invite your mom to jump in.

Laugh out loud. Climb a tree. Take a bubble bath. Count your teeth with your tongue. Chew a wad of gum and pop the bubble on your face. Smell a freshly mowed lawn. Better yet, visit the biggest library in town, stand in the center, and take a long, slow whiff. Inhale the fragrance of thoughts and wisdom. Breaths of library air should cost a quarter each. So get what you can now—free—while the supply lasts.

Walk on a brick wall and sing "Amazing Grace." Sit on your roof and watch the sun set. After it's down, make some popcorn and return for the second show: fireflies at dusk. They're more magical than anything Steven Spielberg or Disneyland can produce.

You want extravagance? I'll give you extravagance. Before you go to bed tonight, talk to God. Don't just mumble a few bless 'ems. Really pray. While you're at it, thank God for sunsets and fireflies and bubble baths. Not to forget babies and popcorn . . . and alarms that don't ring.

See also: Psalm 69:32; 118:24; Luke 10:38–42; Romans 5:17

MORE EXTRAVAGANCE

I commend the enjoyment of life.

ECCLESIASTES 8:15

So you think you can handle two straight days of extravagant pleasure? Aren't you getting a bit carried away? This much pleasure is only for those who are mature. No kids allowed. If you can handle it, cut loose again:

Spend an hour reading French poetry—especially if you can't read French. Pretend you're a taco. Skip down the street backward. Write a letter to your grandparents. Change your bed sheets. Pound a nail with a banana.

Volunteer—it doesn't matter what for. Burp as loud as possible. Fly a kite. In the absence of a strong wind, lie flat on your back and watch the clouds. Pick out faces of people you know in the cottony billows and pray for them before they turn into sheep.

Go to a baseball game. If it's not the season, just buy some peanuts and Cracker Jack. Toss an occasional piece in the air, and catch it in your mouth. Chalk your initials (together with those of a special friend) inside a heart on the sidewalk. If your friend is with you, chalk up a hopscotch game and have a go at it. Try to catch a butterfly. Try to catch each other.

Suck a lemon. It may not strike you as pleasure, but it'll put you in touch with your senses and remind you that you're *alive*. Putting an ice cube down your pants will do the same thing.

Fill up a birdbath. Feed your dog a cookie. If you've never seen a dog smile, feed it another and wait five seconds. Change into your shorts and wash someone else's car. Don't be particular—any old car on the block will do.

Before going to sleep, get your Bible down off your shelf. Dust it off and lay it beside your bed, within reach. Turn off the alarm. When you wake up, thank God for time—and for enabling you to enjoy it. And then ask him for a special day. Ask him to begin by leading you to a special verse in the Bible.

See also: Psalm 16:11; 100; Ecclesiastes 2:26; John 10:10

HOW MUCH LONGER?

No one knows about that day or hour, not even the angels in heaven, nor the Son, but only the Father. As it was in the days of Noah, so it will be at the coming of the Son of Man. For in the days before the flood, people were eating and drinking, marrying and giving in marriage, up to the day Noah entered the ark; and they knew nothing

about what would happen until the flood came and took
them all away. That is how it will be at the coming of the
Son of Man.

MATTHEW 24:36–39

When I was a kid, time seemed to drag in slow motion. On long car trips, my parents tried to quiet me by playing stupid license plate games or seeing who could spot the next Holiday Inn billboard. But I would have none of it. "How much longer?" I'd whine. The response I wanted was, "Soon, very soon."

I'm still time conscious, except now I have my own watch. It tells me when to get up, go to meetings, and when to head home. It indicates how much time is left in class and when the minister will finish his sermon. "How much longer?" A glance at my watch will tell me.

However, watches are useless when it comes to distant events. In determining how much longer till, say, my birthday or Christmas, I consult the calendar.

But neither a watch nor a calendar will help when it comes to determining how much longer till the most momentous event to occur since Jesus visited earth: his second coming. The Bible stresses repeatedly that Christ will return. But you're wasting time if you check a watch or calendar. The Bible just says to be ready.

On our family car trips, we often left in the middle of the night. So when I went to bed, I slept in my clothes. I didn't want to fumble around in my pj's for a half hour. I wanted to be *ready*.

That same level of preparedness also ought to mark our attitude toward Christ's long-heralded second coming. We ought to live in anticipation that it could happen tomorrow. Or, for that matter, today. Our hearts should be ready; our lives in order.

"How much longer?" If Christ were to answer that question, I like to think he'd respond, "Soon, my child, very soon."

See also: Acts 1:7–11; 1 Thessalonians 4:13–5:11

POINTS TO PONDER: TIME

Dear friends, now we are children of God, and what we will be has not yet been made known. But we know that when he appears, we shall be like him, for we shall see him as he is. Everyone who has this hope in him purifies himself, just as he is pure.

1 JOHN 3:2–3

Every experience God gives us, every person he puts in our lives, is the perfect preparation for the future that only he can see.

CORRIE TEN BOOM

Each of us has a capacity for God and an ability to relate to him in a personal way. When we do, he brings to us pardon for the past, peace for the present, and a promise for the future.

RALPH S. BELL

Enjoy the little things, for one day you may look back and realize they were the big things.

ROBERT BRAULT

No man ever sank under the burden of the day. It is when tomorrow's burden is added to the burden of today that the weight is more than a man can bear. Never load yourself so. If you find yourself so loaded, at least remember this: it is your own doing, not God's. He begs you to leave the future to him, and mind the present.

GEORGE MACDONALD

What we are is God's gift to us. What we become is our gift to God.

ELEANOR POWEL

The future has a habit of suddenly and dramatically becoming the present.

ROGER W. BABSON

I said to the man who stood at the gate of the year: Give me a light that I may tread safely into the unknown. And he replied: Go out into the darkness, and put thine hand into the hand of God. That shall be to thee better than light and safer than a known way.

M. LOUISE HASKINS

Lost, yesterday, somewhere between sunrise and sunset, two golden hours, each set with sixty diamond minutes. No reward is offered, for they are gone forever.

HORACE MANN

Those who make the worst use of their time are the first to complain of its shortness.

JEAN DE LA BRUYERE

Many are always praising the bygone time, for it is natural that the old should extol the days of their youth; the weak, the time of their strength; the sick, the season of their vigor; and the disappointed, the springtide of their hopes.

CALEB BINGHAM

I tell you the past is a bucket of ashes.

CARL SANDBURG

It is said that sheep may get lost simply by nibbling away at the grass and never looking up. That can be true for any of us. We can focus so much on what is immediately before us that we fail to see life in larger perspective.

REV. DONALD BITSBERGER

If you can spend a perfectly useless afternoon in a perfectly useless manner, you have learned how to live.

LIN YUTANG

We all find time to do what we really want to do.

WILLIAM FEATHER

Enjoy the blessings of this day, if God sends them; and the evils of it bear patiently and sweetly: for this day only is ours, we are dead to yesterday, and we are not yet born to the morrow.

JEREMY TAYLOR

Throughout the whole [New Testament] there runs the conviction that the time looked forward to by the prophets has in fact arrived in history with the advent of Jesus Christ ... The time of Jesus is *kairos*—a time of opportunity. To embrace the opportunity means salvation; to neglect it, disaster. There is no third course.

JOHN MARSH

Does thou love life? Then do not squander time, for that is the stuff life is made of.

BENJAMIN FRANKLIN

We are so little reconciled to time that we are even astonished at it. "How he's grown!" we exclaim, "How time flies!" as though the universal form of our experience were again and again a novelty. It is as strange as if a fish were repeatedly surprised at the wetness of water. And that would be strange indeed; unless of course the fish were destined to become, one day, a land animal.

C. S. LEWIS

See also: Ecclesiastes 3:1–8; Jeremiah 29:11; Matthew 6:25–34; 2 Corinthians 6:2

WEEK 7

DOUBLESPEAK

If you live according to the sinful nature, you will die; but if by the Spirit you put to death the misdeeds of the body, you will live, because those who are led by the Spirit of God are sons of God.

ROMANS 8:13–14

I once interviewed a TV personality who was often described in the press as being "outspoken" and "ruddy-faced." I didn't know exactly what to expect, but I soon found out. It was a nice way of saying the man was an abusive drunk.

A nice way of saying negative things is what I call *fuzzifying*. For example, the Pentagon fuzzifies when it uses the term *sunshine units* as a measure of nuclear radiation; it's when the president institutes *revenue enhancements* instead of raising taxes. Fuzzifying is what happens when we call war *pacification*, or name the MX missile *Peacekeeper*. That makes as much sense as calling the guillotine a headache remedy.

This linguistic camouflage is seen in the recent slaughter of eight million chickens that were spreading an influenza virus throughout Pennsylvania. The Feds stepped in and gassed them all. When they finally announced what happened, they fuzzified. They said they *depopulated* the birds.

We often fuzzify what the Bible calls s-i-n. The little word sounds too offensive, too harsh, too judgmental. So instead we talk about our "weaknesses," the "things we can't help," our "shortcomings," our "natural inclinations." And so sin flourishes because we treat it like a head cold instead of a cancer.

A rose by any other name may smell just as sweet. And so it is with rattlesnakes and sin. By any other name they're just as lethal. Even in this age of fuzzifying, the wages of "things we can't help" haven't changed a dime.

See also: Ezekiel 18:5–32; Romans 5:17; 6:23; Galatians 6:7–8

EQUAL TREATMENT

Love your neighbor as yourself.

MARK 12:31

Loving other people is practically the hardest thing you can ever do. It's right up there in difficulty with trying to stop lusting, kicking the tobacco habit, not making fun of beach geeks, or eating all of your brussels sprouts.

Loving others is hard because we're all basically "me-oriented." That's why Jesus gave us a tip on how to love people more effectively. He said to love 'em like you love yourself. In other words:

Are you as interested in them as you are in the menu at Wendy's when you're starved?

Do you give them the attention you give your nose upon discovering a zit the day before a big date?

Do you feel the same glow for them as you feel when the cop gives you a warning instead of a ticket?

Do you share with them the joy you reserve for a night out with friends?

Do you have the same compassion for their pain as you do for yourself when your finger is slammed in the car door?

Are you as enthusiastic about them as you are about getting paid?

Do you fuss over them as much as you fuss over your hair before heading for the mall?

Do you feel the same pride in their achievements as you do when you receive a good grade in a tough class?

Do you guard their secrets as jealously as you do your measurements?

Do you have the same level of honesty with them as you do when you look square into the bathroom mirror?

Do you pray for them as much as you pray when you're in BIG trouble?

When it comes right down to it, we're all pretty lousy at loving others. Perhaps that's mostly due to the fact that we love ourselves so much. God doesn't want you to love yourself any less. He just wants you to love others to the same degree.

See also: Romans 13:9; 1 Corinthians 13; 1 John 4:7–21

THE TRUTH ABOUT PHONIES

The heart is deceitful above all things.

JEREMIAH 17:9

In rummaging through the garage recently, I found a box filled with old school newspapers. One of them contained my picture, coupled with a brief interview. What struck me most was my response when asked about my greatest dislike. My answer was brief and to the point: "I can't stand phonies."

How profoundly original. I might just as well have said I couldn't stand warm Coke or dents in my car door. *Everybody* dislikes fakes. Though there's fraud and deceit in all of us, it's just a lot easier to spot in other people. But who's fooling whom?

You misjudge a fly ball and it drops safely at your side. For the next half hour you cover yourself by telling everybody you lost it in the sun.

You're in a grocery store and somebody waves. You wave back and smile . . . until you realize you've never seen the person before in your life. At that point you just pretend to be scratching your head.

Ten minutes after you arrive home from an evening out, your mother stops by your bedroom to ask how things went. You don't feel like rehashing the night, so you pretend you've fallen asleep.

A friend who's been sick asks you how church was on Sunday. You say it was OK—even though you slept in and watched a football game instead.

These are all little wrongs that don't really hurt anybody. That's probably what Ananias and Sapphira thought when they sold some of their property for the church. They reported a smaller selling price and kept some of the money for themselves. Nobody else really knew the difference. But God knew their hypocrisy, and struck them dead on the spot.

In others we call such double-dealing hypocrisy. We call them fakes. In ourselves, well ... it pretty much goes overlooked. We seldom face up to the fact that, apart from God, we're all as phony as three-dollar bills.

See also: Psalm 119:29; Acts 5:1–11; James 1:26

THIEF IN THE NIGHT

Now, brothers, about times and dates we do not need to write to you, for you know very well that the day of the Lord will come like a thief in the night. While people are saying, "Peace and safety," destruction will come on them suddenly, as labor pains on a pregnant woman, and they will not escape. But you, brothers, are not in darkness so that this day should surprise you like a thief.

1 THESSALONIANS 5:1–4

A lot of our neighbors are spooked these days. There's been a rash of break-ins and burglaries, and everybody's skittish because the thief hasn't been caught. He moves quickly and is out before you know he's in. But when you look around the next morning, your VCR, stereo, and most of your valuables are gone.

I don't like surprises, so we keep a dog. I've never been a particular animal lover—in part because a cat I once had always delivered her litters in my desk drawer, and I got tired of wiping slime off my geometry textbook. But I put up with our dog because it barks at people who do suspicious things near our house at night.

In the Bible, Christ's second coming is described as something that will happen like a thief in the night. That's an odd word picture; it brings to mind missing stereos. But if something disappears, it won't be your CD player and speakers. Christ will only take his children. Christians will go to sleep on one side of eternity and wake up face-to-face with Jesus. It will be that quick—"in a flash, in the twinkling of an eye," the Bible says in 1 Corinthians 15:52.

In other words, it's not something you can prepare for at the last minute. And if you're not ready, don't think a guard dog will alert you.

See also: Matthew 24; 2 Peter 3:3–18

TIME OF ARRIVAL

In my Father's house are many rooms; if it were not so, I would have told you. I am going there to prepare a place for you. And if I go and prepare a place for you, I will come back and take you to be with me that you also may be where I am.

JOHN 14:2–3

You read yesterday of Christ's return to earth—an event which will occur as suddenly and unexpectedly as "a thief in the night." That day, known as the Second Coming, was something Christ promised during his last days on earth. He wanted people to know he wasn't ditching them. He would return to take them home. The promise bears his stamp of approval, so you can stake your life on it. In fact, if you *don't* stake your life on it, you are, quite literally, a damned fool.

Nearly two thousand years have passed since Christ talked about coming back and snatching us away to spend the rest of eternity together in heaven. He didn't say when that date would be; he just urged us to live in anticipation of it at all times.

When I first became a Christian, I thought the Second Coming would occur within the next couple of years. But I secretly hoped Christ would at least wait until after I got my driver's license. Then I fell in love, and began to hope he'd hold off until after the wedding night . . . and then until after I had children . . . and then until I had some money in the bank.

Now, however, I hope Christ returns sometime very soon. I still have a lot of goals and ambitions, dreams and desires. Nothing has changed in that department. What has changed is my intense desire to meet Christ face-t-face. There's also another reason: I am tired.

I am tired of the struggle of the Christian life, of the daily battle with lust and pride and jealousy and nagging habits. I've grown weary of looking out for myself, making excuses when I hurt other people, and apologizing when I blurt unkind words. I am tired of Satan's whispers. Most of all, I'm tired of asking forgiveness from the one I love most.

That is why, when I wake in the morning, the first thought on my still-sleepy mind is, "Come soon, Lord Jesus." For all these years he's been preparing a place for us, and I imagine it's getting to be quite a mansion.

I know the homecoming date is near—and that any day now we'll hear the trumpets blow.

See also: Acts 1:10–11; 1 Thessalonians 4:13–18

A DEATH EXPERIENCE

Do not be deceived: God cannot be mocked. A man reaps what he sows. The one who sows to please his sinful nature, from that nature will reap destruction; the one who sows to please the Spirit, from the Spirit will reap eternal life.

GALATIANS 6:7–8

Buried in the shadows of Paul's closet is a large box brimming with cards and letters. Each contains some variable of "I love you" expressed a hundred different ways by his girlfriend Denise. Their love seemed Hallmark perfect ... until she got pregnant and, against his wishes, had an abortion. And now, the letters have stopped coming.

"The abortion was like a death experience," Paul told me, "and I'm still trying to recover. I still think about what it would have been like to have a son—teaching him to ride a bike or play ball. Or I wonder about having a daughter—taking her to ballet lessons, buying her pretty dresses, kissing her good night.

"Most people probably think that when a guy finds out his girlfriend is pregnant, all he wants to do is pay a few hundred bucks for an abortion and never think about it again," Paul continued. "But some days I can think of nothing else. I wanted the child. I wanted to get married. I told Denise I'd do whatever it took to make a home for her and the baby.

"But the people at the clinic had an easier solution. They told her abortion was really no big deal—it was just like removing a 'little glob of tissue.' Maybe it's easier to kill something if you think of it like that," Paul said. "But that 'little glob of tissue' had a heartbeat. It was my child. And my child would have been three on October eleventh ..."

It was difficult listening to Paul because I knew the roots of pain went clear to his bones. I also knew, as did Paul, that the baby never would have been conceived had Paul maintained his relationship with God. But he scrapped his beliefs when Denise entered the picture.

At any point God's forgiveness could be extended to him for the asking. "Though your sins are like scarlet, they shall be as white as snow," says Isaiah. Paul's sins (and Denise's, too) could be erased easily, as they can with any of us. But God's forgiveness doesn't always erase the consequences of sin. Paul's lonely, very painful thoughts about his child are proof of that.

See also: Psalm 139:13–16; Romans 6:11–13; 1 Corinthians 6:18–19

POINTS TO PONDER: GUILT

> *Let us draw near to God with a sincere heart in full assurance of faith, having our hearts sprinkled to cleanse us from a guilty conscience and having our bodies washed with pure water.*

> HEBREWS 10:22

Every man is guilty of all the good he didn't do.

VOLTAIRE

The one thing that doesn't abide by majority rule is a person's conscience.

HARPER LEE

I think I may have to go through the agony of hearing all my sins recited in the presence of God. But I believe it will be like this— Jesus will come over and lay his hand across my shoulders and say to God, "Yes, all these things are true, but I'm here to cover up for

Peter. He is sorry for all his sins, and by a transaction made between us, I am now solely responsible for them."

PETER MARSHALL

We sometimes pretend our conscience doesn't speak our language or is too quiet to hear. No, there's no language barrier and the volume is louder than a train whistle. It's not that we can't understand it or don't hear it; we just choose not to heed it.

S. RICKLY CHRISTIAN

Remorse: beholding heaven and feeling hell.

GEORGE MOORE

Humanity is never so beautiful as when praying for forgiveness, or else forgiving another.

JEAN PAUL RICHTER

It is about as hard to absolve yourself of your own guilt as it is to sit in your own lap. Wrongdoing sparks guilt sparks wrongdoing ad nauseam, and we all try to disguise the grim process from both ourselves and everybody else. In order to break the circuit we need somebody before whom we can put aside the disguise, trusting that when he sees us for what we fully are, he won't run away screaming with, if nothing worse, laughter.

FREDERICK BUECHNER

If his conditions are met, God is bound by his Word to forgive any man or any woman of any sin because of Christ.

BILLY GRAHAM

Conscience—the only incorruptible thing about us.

HENRY FIELDING

The only tyrant I accept in this world is the still voice within.

MAHATMA GANDHI

If we are sinners forgiven, we ought to behave as forgiven, welcomed home, crowned with wonderful love in Christ, and so cheer and encourage all about us, who often go heavily because we reflect our gloom upon them instead of our grateful love, hope, confidence.

FATHER CONGREVE

Remorse is the pain of sin.

THEODORE PARKER

There is no better feeling than to wake up on Sunday morning and be able to face yourself in the mirror. The ability to sleep soundly and then look yourself square in the eye after a Saturday night is life's truest reward.

S. RICKLY CHRISTIAN

See also: John 9:39–41; Romans 7:15–25; James 2:8–10

WEEK 8

A REASON TO LIVE

As he went along, he saw a man blind from birth.
His disciples asked him, "Rabbi, who sinned, this man or
his parents, that he was born blind?"

"Neither this man nor his parents sinned," said
Jesus, "but this happened so that the work of God might
be displayed in his life."

JOHN 9:1–3

Harold's bed was surrounded by get-well wishes, but he was so weak from cancer treatments that he left the envelopes untouched. Finally, on a good day, he opened a letter from a young woman in New Jersey. "I am praying for you," she said. It was signed, Crystal Lavelle.

After exchanging several more letters, she wrote, "If you send me your picture, I'll send you mine." He complied, and then waited expectantly for her next envelope. He pictured her as having long blonde hair and blue eyes, but when her picture arrived he got the surprise of his life. Crystal was in a wheelchair, her body and legs twisted by cerebral palsy.

In an accompanying note, she explained that she'd been born with the disease. Eventually, Harold learned that her parents, who had become wealthy through business, had given her up at birth and she'd spent her life in institutions. But God replaced her bitterness toward them with love. He also gave her a reason to live: she wanted to see her parents meet her Savior.

Toward that goal, Crystal spends six hours every day at work—screwing nuts and bolts together. All year she saves her nickels and dimes for a plane ticket to visit her parents and tell them Jesus loves them. She also visits local high schools, telling young people how God transformed her life.

One night Crystal called Harold late at night. His cancer was in remission and he was feeling better. But Crystal said she wasn't doing well and asked him to pray for her. And so he did, right there on the phone, asking God to free her from the wheelchair. But she promptly cut him off.

"No, Harold," she said. "The wheelchair is my pulpit, my ministry. I am freer in this chair than most people who have complete use of their bodies. I don't have legs, but I've got Jesus. And he's all I need."

That night Harold witnessed genuine faith, which helped him cope with his own serious problems. In Crystal he saw a woman who had never climbed a tree, pedaled a bike, or experienced the love of her parents. But she knew the love of God clear to her bones.

She also knew God could heal her with a snap of his fingers. But she didn't want that for one reason: Were she to be healed, her pulpit would be empty.

See also: Hebrews 11; James 5:13–16

SUBSTITUTE MOM

If anyone wants to be first, he must be the very last, and the servant of all.

MARK 9:35

As the saying goes, behind all great people there is a woman. Yesterday you read about Crystal, who radiates greatness if only because she believes in a great God. But is there a woman who stands behind Crystal? Yes. Her name is Mary Sue.

Most people would not look twice at Mary Sue. Her clothes are worn, she is elderly, she is black. On her tired hands and feet are calluses and bunions of Rocky Mountain proportions. They mark her lifetime of service.

One of fifteen children, Mary Sue mothered seven of her younger brothers and sisters when her own mother died. Then came a bad marriage, the birth of a handicapped son, nonstop work, and sleepless nights. She supports her family and extended family by doing what she does at home: caring for people. For more than twenty years, she has been the mother Crystal never had, and has loved her day by day as she grew from a child to an adult.

Mary Sue arrives at Crystal's institution about the same time as the first light of dawn, and spends most of her time in the kitchen making all the meals for Crystal and the other fifteen residents. When Mary Sue isn't mixing and frying and scrubbing and sweeping, she sits in a corner beside Crystal, talking gently and stroking her hair. Her eyes fairly glow.

In the evening, she returns home to her grandchildren and severely handicapped son to draw baths and chase everybody off to bed while she tends house long into the night.

Mary Sue doesn't do what she does for a material reward; there is none. She is driven solely by love and a desire to serve. If there is a bonus, it is the chance to hear Crystal sing in her twisted but happy voice, "Jesuh, I 'ove 'ou. I 'ove 'ou with all my 'eart. Jesuh, I 'ove 'ou. I give 'ou my all!"

Mary Sue's love is the love of Christ, displayed in very ordinary, everyday ways. And though most people wouldn't notice her on the street, I know there is a special corner in heaven waiting for her ... and for those among us who would follow Christ by following her example.

See also: Mark 10:35–45; Philippians 2:3–8

THE ARRANGEMENT

Children, obey your parents in the Lord, for this is right. "Honor your father and mother"—which is the first commandment with a promise—"that it may go well with you and that you may enjoy long life on the earth."

EPHESIANS 6:1–3

Imagine the scenario. You've just returned home from school, and all you want to do is plop down on the bed, crank up the stereo, and think about your close encounter with Blue Eyes. But there's a car in the driveway, and you swallow hard. Forget the dreams—your parents are interviewing to find you a spouse.

For the past several months, they have scoured their social circles for potential match-ups. And now they've finally settled on Chris, who's not exactly *ugly* but is not in the same league as Blue Eyes. Not that anybody's asked your opinion, but . . . the kid's got braces and Snow White legs! Not to mention that you don't even go to the same school and have only seen each other once before at that stupid Parent/Kid club your parents joined when they were hunting for a wife for your big brother.

Over the next eight years, you and Chris see each other only twice, and when you finally get married and move in together, you are virtual strangers. But you have no choice, so you force yourself to make the best of things.

This scenario may seem pretty absurd, although over half of all marriages in the world today are still arranged. But every day you have to deal with a situation that's not all that different. You've got to share living quarters with a group of people you did not personally select: your family.

Generally speaking, you didn't pick your parents; they didn't pick you. The same is true of any siblings you may have. And if you're like most families, the mix of personalities, individual needs, and daily demands can be both interesting and explosive.

Chances are, your parents don't understand some pretty basic things about you. Nevertheless, God asks that you honor and obey them—in essence, *love* them. Why? Perhaps because "getting along" is such a tremendous need in the world. Maybe if we'd all practice more at home, our own little corner of the world would improve. That's not an easy task. But with dogged effort—and a great deal of grace—it can be done.

See also: Proverbs 6:20–22; Colossians 3:20; 2 Timothy 3:1–2

BRIDGING THE GAP

Listen, my son, to your father's instruction and do not forsake your mother's teaching.

PROVERBS 1:8

Do you sometimes feel your parents are aliens? That your mother is from Mars and your father is from Pluto? That they don't understand a thing about you? But how much do *you* really know about *them*, other than that they're old and wear funny swimsuits?

In spite of all of your differences, ask God to help you better understand your parents. Toward that goal, sit your parents (one will do) down tonight, and get them to respond to the following mini-questionnaire. Their answers may surprise you and also may open up some new lines of communication.

1. Tell me one funny thing that happened to you growing up.
2. Tell me one thing you did wrong as a kid for which you never got caught. Honesty counts ten points.
3. What's your favorite ice cream flavor?
4. Describe a typical day for you when I'm at school—what do you actually do?
5. Tell me about when you met Mom (or Dad). How old were you when you got married? Why did you get married?
6. Who was the first person you ever kissed? Describe the scene, with all of the juicy details. Who initiated it?
7. Describe your two closest friends when you were my age.
8. Which do you like better, sunrise or sunset? Why?
9. What did you always want to be when you grew up?

10. Did you ever have a boss you didn't particularly like?
11. What really bugs you?
12. Tell me about something you've done that really makes you proud.
13. Which do you like better, Saturdays or Sundays? Why?
14. Which emotion is the hardest for you to express? Why?
15. If you knew you were going to die tomorrow, what would you want to say to me today?

If you want to really do this interview right, tape the conversation, or better yet, shoot it on video. Messing with all the equipment may be a hassle, and you can probably think of fifteen reasons *not* to do it. But do it anyway. And for once, forget that your parents are your parents. Think of them as real, live people who possibly, just maybe, might have something interesting to say.

Oh, and hang on to the tape. Tuck it away someplace safe. Ten years from now it will be worth its weight in gold.

See also: Ecclesiastes 7:25; Luke 2:41–52

TIME TRAVELS

> *Show me, O Lord, my life's end and the number of my days; let me know how fleeting is my life. You have made my days a mere handbreadth; the span of my years is as nothing before you. Each man's life is but a breath.*
>
> **PSALM 39:4–5**

Mrs. Simone once loved life. But that was before her last slip in the tub when something clicked in her brain; before she started spending all day in bed, refusing to look out the window; before she began her time travels.

"Where's Daddy?" she demanded when I walked in the room. "He should be home by now."

109

"He's dead," I said as calmly as possible. "Remember?"

She didn't, of course. Daddy was her husband, who'd passed away ten years earlier. It was only in the past couple of months that she'd forgotten he was gone. We used to talk about him on Sundays when I'd visit her and other nursing home residents after church.

I was at the home once when her only son stopped by. He walked over to her side and kissed her on the cheek. She drew back, as if he had a horrible, infectious disease.

"Who are you?" she asked.

"Robert," he said quietly.

She shook her head. "Robert's this big," she said, holding her veiny hand about three feet from the floor.

"I'm Robert, Mom," he tried again, combing his fingers through his hair, which was gray at the sides. The pain of having a mother who did not recognize him showed on his face.

"Did I tell you what Libby Briggs said today at the parlor?" she asked this stranger-son standing beside her.

"Libby died fifteen years ago, Mom," he replied.

"Close the door, you're letting the flies in," she said abruptly.

I don't know what he was thinking as he stood there carrying on this sad and silly conversation. But I imagine his brain was racing—thinking back on all the good times they shared; the times when he actually *was* three feet high and needed his mother like he needed his next breath; the times when his mother was young and vivacious and caring; the times when getting out of the tub was as easy for her as brushing her teeth; the times before her time travels.

That all probably seemed like yesterday to him as he searched his mother's porcelain face for any sign of recognition. But there was none, not even a glimmer. Though her body was still alive, the woman he'd grown up calling Mom and who'd made all those special memories possible was gone. She'd disappeared, as if her life was but a breath of air, which is exactly what life is.

Unable to do anything else but love this poor shell of a mother that used to be, he leaned over and kissed her lightly. When he turned to leave, he had tears in his eyes.

See also: Job 14:2; Ecclesiastes 3:1–2; 12:1

A PLACE CALLED HOME

Above all, love each other deeply, because love covers over a multitude of sins.

1 PETER 4:8

When I think of family, I think a lot about the home I grew up in. It was situated on a sleepy cul-de-sac in San Diego, just around the corner from a huge canyon where we caught lizards and built forts, and a short block from the elementary school where I learned the true meaning of the words *vice principal.* On a map it was located at 8891 Armorss Avenue.

Of course, home was more than an address or the material used to build it. Home was *family*, without which it would have been just another house. And oh, what a family we were!

We were a pretty diverse bunch, consisting of a Mr. Good-wrench father, who could fix just about anything but broken dreams; a Betty Crocker mother who made sense of stock market tables as easily as she made good meals; a goody-goody sister who befriended teachers as easily as boys; and a daredevil brother who wasn't happy unless he was breaking his bones.

We all generally got along, except when we didn't. That is, we had our share of differences which sometimes erupted into top-of-the-lungs fights. One or the other of us may have even threatened on occasion to pull the other's tongue out. But we all survived, even prospered, because the words "I love you" were expressed daily in our home and because it was always very clear that my dad loved my

111

mother, my mother loved my dad, and together they loved each of us kids. That love enabled us to overlook our differences and thrive as a family—through sickness and health, births and deaths, successes and failures.

In recent years, we've all gone our separate ways, and the old home was finally sold. But each of us remains linked to the others by our common heritage and bond of love, together with all of the memories and good times and joys we shared at that place called home.

As John Henry Jowett points out, "The Bible does not say very much about homes; it says a great deal about the things that make them. It speaks about life and love and joy and peace and rest. If we get a house and put these into it, we shall have secured a home."

And that's what I had: a home *secured* by all that God intended. It was, truly, a foretaste of heaven, an interpretation of what will one day be our Home of homes.

See also: Proverbs 3:33; 10:12; Ephesians 6:1–3

POINTS TO PONDER: FAMILY AND HOME

> *Honor your father and your mother, so that you may live long in the land the Lord your God is giving you.*
>
> EXODUS 20:12

The family you come from isn't as important as the family you're going to have.

RING LARDNER

All happy families resemble one another; every unhappy family is unhappy in its own way.

LEO TOLSTOY

Children aren't happy with nothing to ignore, And that's what parents were created for.

OGDEN NASH

My parents taught me how to put one foot before the other, how to balance on a bike, and how to work the gear shift of an automobile. But when they gave me my first Bible, I discovered I had wings.

S. RICKLY CHRISTIAN

The most important thing a father can do for his children is to love their mother.

THEODORE M. HESBURGH

Home is where the heart is.

PLINY THE ELDER

The words that a father speaks to his children in the privacy of home are not heard by the world, but, as in whispering-galleries, they are clearly heard at the end of posterity.

JEAN PAUL RICHTER

God could not be everywhere, and therefore he made mothers.

JEWISH PROVERB

A family is a unit composed not only of children but of men, women, an occasional animal, and the common cold.

OGDEN NASH

A happy family is but an earlier heaven.

JOHN BOWRING

Home interprets heaven. Home is heaven for beginners.

CHARLES H. PARKHURST

Everybody believes divorce breaks up families. This is not so. The broken family is not the result of divorce; divorce is the result of the broken family.

PAUL W. ALEXANDER

Heaven will be the perfection we have always longed for. All the things that made earth unlovely and tragic will be absent in heaven. There will be no night, no death, no disease, no sorrow, no tears, no ignorance, no disappointment, no war. It will be filled with health, vigor, virility, knowledge, happiness, worship, love, and perfection.

BILLY GRAHAM

Every father expects his boy to do the things he wouldn't do when he was young.

KIN HUBBARD

The first half of our lives is ruined by our parents and the second half by our children.

CLARENCE DARROW

It is dangerous to confuse children with angels.

DAVID FYFE

Domestic happiness depends upon the ability to overlook.

ROY L. SMITH

See also: Proverbs 1:7–8; Acts 16:31–34

WEEK
9

QUIET ME, LORD

The Lord your God is with you, he is mighty to save. He will take great delight in you, he will quiet you with his love.

ZEPHANIAH 3:17

Quiet me, Lord,
From the crash-boom-bam noise of life
That overpowers my ears like the slamming of locker doors,
The blare of stereos,
The honk of traffic,
The scream of revenge.

Slow me, Lord,
From the hit-and-run pace of life
That overwhelms my peace like the breathlessness of time,
The blur of yesterday,
The rush of today,
The press of tomorrow.

Relax me, Lord,
From the knot-in-the-gut tension of life,
That stews my insides like the strain of broken friendship,
The grind of ambition,
The ulcer of bad habits,
The gnaw of hormones.

Shelter me, Lord,
From the haymaker-to-the-head blows of life
That assault my strength like the slap of old memories,
The sting of sharp words,
The clash of competing motives,
The dig of gossip.

Quiet me with your love, Lord,
Slow me with your patience,
Relax me with your peace,
Shelter me with your Spirit.
But most of all, Lord,
Overwhelm
me
with
you.

See also: Psalm 46:10; John 14:27; Galatians 5:22

RESOLUTIONS

> *Strengthen your feeble arms and weak knees. "Make level paths for your feet," so that the lame may not be disabled, but rather healed. Make every effort to live in peace with all men and to be holy; without holiness no one will see the Lord. See to it that no one misses the grace of God and that no bitter root grows up to cause trouble and defile many. See that no one is sexually immoral, or is godless.*
>
> **HEBREWS 12:12–16**

At the start of every year I retreat from the rush of everyday concerns and think about what might have been and what might yet be. Sometimes I even write out resolutions.

Consider adopting the following list. It works just as well in the middle of the year as on January 1. If you faithfully adhere to it week after week, you will end up with the year of your life.

1. I will gain no more than 2.3 percent of my body
   weight in pimples, unless I give up Big Macs and fries,

117

which is obviously something I won't do . . . even if I could.

2. Once and for all, no matter what, by the grace of God, I will kick the _____ habit. (Fill in the blank, unless your parents snoop.)

3. I won't write run-on sentences they are hard to read.

4. I will surprise my parents and thank each of them for something, *anything*, once a week for at least five weeks, even if they snoop and deserve hard labor in upper Siberia.

5. I will never admit that I swish Jell-O between my teeth, unless in confidence to fellow swishers.

6. I will make every effort to smile at somebody I'd rather not smile at—for at least the next seven times I see them.

7. I will volunteer for no more than two extracurricular assignments per week that I have no intention of doing.

8. I will remind myself overandoverandover again that God loves me—even if I still haven't kicked the _____ habit, which I'll do, doggone it, if it's the *last* thing I do.

9. I will not spend money frivolously, except for cherry Jell-O.

10. I will read the Bible verse at the beginning of each day's reading in this book (Does the one above sound like a New Year's list of sorts?) and also look up and read the verses at the end of every day.

See also: Romans 6:4–7; 2 Corinthians 5:17

MORE RESOLUTIONS

You were taught, with regard to your former way of life, to put off your old self, which is being corrupted by its deceitful desires; to be made new in the attitude of your minds; and to put on the new self, created to be like God in true righteousness and holiness.

EPHESIANS 4:22–24

Yesterday I mentioned that I start out most new years with the idea of doing things differently. No matter if things are going poorly; every January offers a fresh start. If things are going well, I expect them to get even better. But why wait for January? As the saying goes, today is the first day of the rest of your life.

Review yesterday's list of resolutions, then incorporate the following additions. Tomorrow you can personalize the list by writing some of your own.

1. I will not eat anything fried or containing white flour before 2 P.M., unless I'm absolutely sure I can take a one-hour nap in the library before the end of the school day.
2. I will try for a personal record and see how long I can go without consciously sinning. When I fail, I will immediately 'fess up to God, who honestly cares about these things.
3. I will never again use Lysol as a substitute deodorant.
4. Did I say I'll do everything I can to kick the habit?
5. Even when my teeth feel like a sweater, I will never ever floss in the company or sight of any living creature.
6. I will be more kind, especially to nerds and geeks and gorps and other alien creatures.

7. I won't use no double negatives, or, commas, which aren't necessary.
8. I will eat fewer beans and more frozen yogurt.
9. I will keep my distance from the television, unless it happens to be on. But under no circumstances will I watch anything dealing with dwarf throwing or the mating habits of South American sea slugs.
10. Today, at this very moment, I will claim the power that is mine as a believer. I will actually start living like a Christian and quit just sounding like one.

See also: Isaiah 1:18; Romans 8:18–23

A PERSONAL LIST

What is impossible with men is possible with God.
LUKE 18:27

For the past couple of days we've been looking at implementing changes in our lives. Thankfully, for a Christian, every day can bring a fresh start. As A. W. Criswell said, "Christianity is the land of beginning again."

Now it's your turn to personalize the list. (Ten points for honesty!) When you're done, refer to these combined lists often. And remember, the hardest things to change are the very things God is most eager to help you with. As the verse above indicates, his business is turning your impossibilities into possibilities.

1. I've been putting it off for months (years, if the truth were known), but the time is finally right to try to

   _____.

2. When it comes to my relationships with the opposite sex, I will, with God's help, do my best to _____.

3. I'm going to quit battling with myself and finally turn _____ over to the Lord, knowing that *nobody* cares as much about the situation as he does.

4. With regard to my family, I will honestly try to _____.

5. The one area of my personality I'd like to work on in the next few weeks is _____.

6. I always seem to open my big mouth at the wrong time and embarrass myself. Lord, help me to zip my lip, especially when _____.

7. I will spend at least _____ minutes alone daily, reading God's Word and honestly talking to him about my concerns.

8. My life would be a whole lot easier if I could just quit _____, which I can do, because "What is impossible with men is possible with God."

9. I'm not asking for body alterations, but I can improve my looks in little ways by _____.

10. Yeoowww! Cowabunga! To get truly excited about my life I will start _____ *today.* Awoooo!

See also: Matthew 19:26; Romans 12:9–21; Hebrews 12:1

I KNOW THE FEELING

All have sinned and fall short of the glory of God.

ROMANS 3:23

Turgenev. Maybe you've heard of him, maybe not. He didn't figure skate or play hockey or sing in a gypsy band. He was a famous Russian novelist. And like most Russians, his first name was Ivan.

Based on something he wrote way back when, I feel a sort of kinship with him. You see, he penned two sentences that I've not been able to get out of my mind: "I don't know what the heart of a bad man is like. But I know what the heart of a good man is like, and it's terrible."

What he was getting at is the same thought the apostle Paul had in mind in the verse above from Romans: failure. It's as if God set a big target on a tree, and we all shoot wide. Not only do we not hit the bull's-eye, we often miss the entire target. Our arrows end up in the dirt, the branches, the bushes—everywhere but where we aim. Simply put, we fail. Not every minute of every day, but often enough to understand failure better than anything else we do.

Failure is the feeling of saying something you regret, of compromising your virtue, of giving in to the same old sin. Failure is the feeling of being overrun by lurid thoughts. It's the feeling of brushing God aside—again.

I know the feeling. So did Turgenev. So did the apostle Paul, as you can tell from his very personal remarks in Romans 7:15-25 (*The Message*):

"What I don't understand about myself is that I decide one way, but then I act another, doing things I absolutely despise. So if I can't be trusted to figure out what is best for myself and then do it, it becomes obvious that God's command is necessary.

"But I need something *more*! For if I know the law but still can't keep it, and if the power of sin within me keeps sabotaging my best intentions, I obviously need help! I realize that I don't have what it takes. I can will it, but I can't *do* it. I decide to do good, but I don't *really* do it; I decide not to do bad, but then I do it anyway. My decisions, such as they are, don't result in actions. Something has gone wrong deep within me and gets the better of me every time.

"It happens so regularly that it's predictable. The moment I decide to do good, sin is there to trip me up. I truly delight in God's commands, but it's pretty obvious that not all of me joins in that delight. Parts of me covertly rebel, and just when I least expect it, they take charge.

"I've tried everything and nothing helps. I'm at the end of my rope. Is there no one who can do anything for me? Isn't that the real question?"

Good question. The poor guy, he sounds just like me. But his answer was even better: "The answer, thank God, is that Jesus Christ can and does. He acted to set things right in this life of contradictions where I want to serve God with all my heart and mind, but am pulled by the influence of sin to do something totally different."

Things haven't changed much in these two thousand years. On our own, we're trapped. Only Jesus Christ can free us from sin's prison. He stands with his hands outstretched, ready to help us off of failure's merry-go-round. Ready to help us start over, to rebuild, to begin again. All we have to do is ask.

See also: Hebrews 4:14–16; Revelation 21:1–4

HEROIC FAILURES

Whatever your hand finds to do, do it with all your might.

ECCLESIASTES 9:10

If you've ever felt you're continually crashing against closed doors and that your dreams are routinely dismissed, don't give up. The following examples, courtesy of Norman Chalfin of the Jet Propulsion Laboratory's Office of Patent Control, indicate that you're in distinguished company:

- When Samuel F. B. Morse asked Congress for a grant to build a telegraph line between Washington, D. C., and Baltimore, he was greeted with derision and suggestions that instead he build "a railroad to the moon."
- Asked by Parliament whether the telephone would be of any use in Britain, the chief engineer of the British Post

Office answered, "No, sir. The Americans have need of the telephone, but we do not. We have plenty of messenger boys."

- H. G. Wells, the visionary British writer, did not think it likely that aeronautics would ever be important in transportation. "Man is not an albatross," he said.
- In 1903, a year before the Wright brothers flew at Kitty Hawk, Prof. Simon Newcomb, a distinguished astronomer, said that flying without a gas bag was impossible, or at least would require the discovery of a new law of nature.
- A week before the Wright brothers' flight, the *New York Times* editorialized on the rival efforts of Samuel Pierpont Langley, who had just achieved flight by an unmanned heavier-than-air craft: "We hope that Prof. Langley will not put his substantial greatness as a scientist in further peril by continuing to waste his time and the money involved in further airship experiments. Life is short and he is capable of services to humanity incomparably greater than trying to fly."

Within three years, the Wrights had an airplane that could fly forty miles an hour for one hundred miles. They offered it to the British navy. The Admiralty declined, explaining that the aeroplane would be of no practical use in the naval service.

If it's mediocrity you're after, it can be had easily. But if you are to attain excellence, no matter what the field, you must work with all of your might. You can't be allergic to sweat. You must also, on occasion at least, thumb your nose at the skeptics around you. They've been wrong before and they'll be wrong again.

See also: Ecclesiastes 11:6; Colossians 3:23

POINTS TO PONDER: FAILURE

Because of the Lord's great love we are not consumed, for his compassions never fail. They are new every morning; great is your faithfulness.

LAMENTATIONS 3:22–23

When I was young I observed that nine out of every ten things I did were failures, so I did ten times more work.

GEORGE BERNARD SHAW

Show me a thoroughly satisfied man and I will show you a failure.

THOMAS EDISON

The only people who never fail are those who never try.

ILKA CHASE

Failure is not sin. Faithlessness is.

HENRIETTA MEARS

Failures are divided into two classes—those who thought and never did, and those who did and never thought.

JOHN CHARLES SALAK

There is no failure so great that a Christian cannot rise from it.

HELEN C. WHITE

It is not a disgrace to fail. Failing is one of the greatest arts in the world.

CHARLES KETTERING

The only time you don't fail is the last time you try anything—and it works.

WILLIAM STRONG

125

I never knew any man in my life who could not bear another's misfortunes perfectly like a Christian.

ALEXANDER POPE

A failure is a man who has blundered but is not able to cash in the experience.

ELBERT HUBBARD

Not failure, but low aim, is crime.

JAMES RUSSELL LOWELL

A man can fail many times, but he isn't a failure until he begins to blame somebody else.

JOHN BURROUGHS

We should strengthen ourselves against these failings: neglect of godliness; study without understanding; failure to act up to what we believe to be right; inability to change bad habits.

CONFUCIUS

Ninety-nine percent of the failures come from people who have the habit of making excuses.

GEORGE WASHINGTON CARVER

One must never confuse error and the person who errs.

POPE JOHN XXIII

Men do not fail; they give up trying.

ELIHU ROOT

I cannot give you the formula for success, but I can give you the formula for failure: Try to please everybody.

HERBERT BAYARD SWOPE

A law of nature rules that energy cannot be destroyed. You change its form from coal to steam, from steam to power in the turbine, but you do not destroy energy. In the same way, another law governs human activity and rules that honest effort cannot be lost, but that some day the proper benefits will be forthcoming.

PAUL SPEICHER

Success has many mothers, but failure is an orphan.

ANONYMOUS

A man should never be ashamed to own he has been in the wrong, which is but saying, in other words, that he is wiser today than he was yesterday.

JONATHAN SWIFT

See also: Proverbs 15:22; 2 Corinthians 6:3–10; 12:9–10; 13:5–7

WEEK

10

GETTING EVEN

Do not take revenge, my friends, but leave room for God's wrath, for it is written: "It is mine to avenge; I will repay," says the Lord. On the contrary: "If your enemy is hungry, feed him; if he is thirsty, give him something to drink. In doing this, you will heap burning coals on his head."

ROMANS 12:19–20

To be quite blunt, I struggle with being warm and loving toward those who have done me wrong. Take for instance the four-wheeling jerk who splashed mud all over my car at the corner of Allegheny and Delmonico in April 1994 when I simply honked at him for parking at a green light. *You know who you are, even after all this time, and if you're that jerk, I hope your radiator blows up!*

See? I'm not quite there yet.

Confession time: I also gloat sometimes when misfortune visits somebody who "deserves it." I once had a boss with major-league arrogance who was a direct descendant of Hitler. His chief ambition was to make me miserable, and in that regard, he was very good at his job. The thing is, he mistreated everybody. And when a whole group of us "crybabies" complained to *his* boss, Hitler Jr. was quietly transferred to an obscure area of the company.

The day I heard the news, I whooped it up like New Year's. A few months later I spotted him across a room. His arm was in a cast. I didn't know how he busted it, nor did I care. All I could think of was that it couldn't have happened to a more deserving guy.

OK, I am aware of the huge disparity between my reaction when wronged and that of Jesus, whose sole response to those who shamed him, flogged him, beat him, and crucified him was: "Father, forgive them, for they do not know what they are doing." He could have wasted the bunch of them. Instead, he died for them, with a prayer for them on his lips.

I don't come close to his standard. I gloat. I bear grudges. I seek revenge. I hate. And that's why he died for me, as well.

See also: Leviticus 19:18; 1 Peter 2:23

TOUGH BREAK, CHUMP

You should not look down on your brother in the day of his misfortune.

OBADIAH 12

Yesterday I gave you a glimpse into my sometimes dirty, withered soul. However, I wasn't completely honest. I didn't go far enough in the tour of my parched heart of hearts.

To continue, sometimes those I've begrudged may not have actually done me wrong. They may have, say, won a scholarship that I thought I really deserved, or slammed a lucky home run when everybody *knows* the guy couldn't hit the side of a barn if he were standing right in front of it. For that matter, maybe they just have a nicer car or get better grades.

Related to all of the above is the pleasure I derive when somebody's misfortune benefits me. This happened once when the father of a kid who was getting too friendly with *my* girlfriend got transferred two thousand miles away. My reaction? Tough break, chump.

There's also the quiet rush I feel when those who live in ivory towers get a taste of real life. For example, I had no trouble sleeping when that goofy televangelist with the big hair got jailed, or on hearing the homecoming queen blimped out after graduation and gained fifty pounds, all in her thighs.

I don't want you to get the wrong idea. I'm actually a terrific guy, whom my mother would describe as warm and sensitive. But deep down I know I fall light years short of the glory of God; so do we all. I am well aware, even if others aren't, that I don't often represent humanity at its best.

My lapses give me a clear picture of my desperate, daily need for a Savior. They also provide an inkling of how certain individuals may feel toward me the next time I fall flat on my face.

See also: Exodus 23:4–5; Matthew 5:44–47; 7:1–5

TRUE LOVE

This is how we know what love is: Jesus Christ laid down his life for us.

1 JOHN 3:16

Boy meets girl, they fall in love. It's the oldest plot around, but it still sells movies, records, and books, along with cosmetics, cars, health club memberships, and most everything else you can imagine except Preparation-H.

However, with all the talk about love in our culture, it's amazingly difficult to define. You can *love* the smell of Opium perfume. You can *love* your main squeeze. You can *love* Julia Roberts' hair. And then, you can *love* God.

You may be unable to easily define love, but chances are you know it when you *feel* it. That's why I found it so difficult as a young Christian to get really excited about God. I expected to *feel* more. When I invited Christ into my heart, I was actually a little disappointed. The way some people talked about their conversion experiences, I expected a major rush. But when the Big Moment arrived, I experienced no celestial surges, no Fourth-of-July fireworks in my toes. I couldn't even raise a goose bump.

Did the absence of stand-up-and-holler emotion mean I wasn't a Christian? It crossed my mind. But over time, I began to understand that my love for God—that is, deeply-rooted, unconditional love—was nothing like the love that's portrayed by Madison Avenue. It was and is a love based not on feelings but on historical *fact*: that Christ died for my sins, that he was buried, and that three days later he was resurrected. Therein lie the roots of true love.

There are days I don't *feel* very Christian; my prayers just seem to bounce off the ceiling. At such times, God feels distant. But the *fact* remains: Because of the cross I can know true love that will last through all eternity. Without the cross, I would get exactly what I deserve: a non-refundable one-way ticket straight to hell.

See also: 1 Corinthians 13; 15:3–5; 1 John 4:19

LOOSE LIPS

Whoever would love life and see good days must keep his tongue from evil and his lips from deceitful speech.

1 PETER 3:10

It didn't seem like such a big deal at first. A young woman casually mentioned that she'd heard somebody had been bitten by a snake when trying on a K-mart coat imported from the Far East. As preposterous as the tale was, it spread crazily throughout the entire Detroit area—and beyond.

Similar nightmarish rumors have circulated often in recent years. False worms-in-the-burgers stories were first directed at Wendy's in Chattanooga, but then latched onto McDonald's as the rumors spread and mutated across the country. Other recent bogus scares included charges that fried chicken companies used batter that caused sterility and served fried rats; that Proctor & Gamble's moon-and-stars logo betrayed a link to devil worship, that Corona Extra was contaminated with urine; that the Moonies controlled Entenmann's Bakery; that major oil companies were dumping gas in the Nevada desert to create a shortage and thereby hike pump prices; and that a Brazilian worker fell into a vat of Coca-Cola and was never retrieved.

Unfortunately, these rumors did not quietly go away. The above-mentioned companies were forced to spend millions of dollars to regain their reputations. But what happens if you're not a corporation? What happens if the rumors are just as preposterous, but are directed toward you, a flesh-and-blood human being? As Joseph Hall said, "A reputation once broken may possibly be repaired, but the world will always keep their eyes on the spot where the crack was."

And so it was with Cindy. One weekend she went to the mall with her cousin Bob, who was several years older. Somebody saw them, and on Monday her friends were oohhing and ahhhing about the hunk they'd heard she was with. A couple of days later people were talking about her new *college boyfriend*. Before long Cindy and her mystery friend were said to be intimate and, well, the stories deteriorated from there. Though she explained over and over what the true story was, every denial was met with smiles and winks.

In the months that followed, Cindy was a wreck. It's fair to say I saw her die emotionally before my eyes. I felt like the witness of a homicide. The murder weapon was a tongue.

See also: Psalm 140:1–3; James 3:5–6

FIRST IMPORTANCE

For what I received I passed on to you as of first importance; that Christ died for our sins according to the Scriptures, that he was buried, that he was raised on the third day according to the Scriptures, and that he appeared to Peter, and then to the Twelve.

1 CORINTHIANS 15:3–5

The Bible is the product of various writers conveying important truths about God, man, life, and the afterlife over several thousand years. Each of the writers had a different message to convey.

Moses brought us the Ten Commandments—an official rule book of morality. King David delivered the Psalms—an intimate songbook that mirrors God's personal relationship with man. King Solomon wrote Ecclesiastes—a despairing look at the meaninglessness of life apart from God. Matthew, Mark, Luke, and John penned the gospels—dramatic narrations of Jesus' life on earth. The apostle Paul gave us much of the New Testament—summaries of the Christian faith for the new church.

In view of the sheer bulk of the Bible, have you ever asked yourself what it all comes down to? What is God really trying to communicate anyway? Can his agenda be condensed to a single verse? Genesis 1:1, maybe? Or perhaps Romans 3:23? The final showdown between God and Satan? What is *most* important?

That was something Paul wrestled with in his letter to the young church at Corinth. What do you tell a group of believers who are struggling to make sense of God amidst all the immorality and materialism around them? Paul's response: "For what I received I passed on to you as of first importance; that Christ died for our sins …"

There you have it: *first importance*. In all God's dealings with man, from Genesis onward, nothing matters more than the cross. Why? Because the very Son of the very Creator of the universe hung there. Nowhere else did God so vividly display his love. Nowhere else did he put it all on the line.

The cross. It was where love mastered evil, where time intersected eternity, where God bridged heaven and earth. The cross. The closer we live to it, the more we truly live.

See also: John 3:16; 1 Corinthians 1:18; 2:2

GOD! LET ME PRAISE YOU

Through Jesus, therefore, let us continually offer to God a sacrifice of praise—the fruit of lips that confess his name. And do not forget to do good and to share with others, for with such sacrifices God is pleased.

HEBREWS 13:15–16

God! Let me praise you
By taking an active role in my corner of your creation,
And filling the area in which I live with
Your light, warmth, love, and happiness.
God! Let me praise you
By brightening the lives of those around me,
And encouraging them with such words as
"I love you," "Thanks," and "I forgive you."
God! Let me praise you
By sharing with others everything you've given me,
And being the first in a group to offer
A smile, hug, condolence, and helping hand.
God! Let me praise you
By fighting back gloom when it surrounds me,
And not being contagious whenever I'm feeling
Discouraged, upset, lonely, and disappointed.
God! Let me praise you
By turning to you at every moment of every day,
And acknowledging your love for me with
My words, actions, thoughts, and prayers.

See also: 2 Corinthians 1:3–4; Ephesians 1:3–14; James 3:9–12

POINTS TO PONDER: PRAISE

Enter his gates with thanksgiving and his courts with praise; give thanks to him and praise his name. For the Lord is good and his love endures forever; his faithfulness continues through all generations.

PSALM 100:4–5

What else can I do, a lame old man, but sing hymns to God? If I were a nightingale, I would do the nightingale's part; if I were a swan, I would do as a swan. But now I am a rational creature, and I ought to praise God: this is my work; I do it, nor will I desert my post, so long as I am allowed to keep it. And I exhort you to join me in this same song.

EPICTETUS

It is a sure sign of mediocrity to be niggardly with praise.

MARQUIS DE VAUVENARGUES

I can live for two months on a good compliment.

MARK TWAIN

Praise God, from whom all blessings flow; Praise Him, all creatures here below; Praise Him above, ye heavenly host; Praise Father, Son, and Holy Ghost.

THOMAS KEN

One thing scientists have discovered is that often-praised children become more intelligent than often-blamed ones. There's a creative element in praise.

THOMAS DREIER

The trouble with most of us is that we would rather be ruined by praise than saved by criticism.

NORMAN VINCENT PEALE

Praise makes good men better and bad men worse.

THOMAS FULLER

If you have never heard the mountains singing, or seen the trees of the field clapping their hands, do not think because of that they don't. Ask God to open your ears so you may hear it, and your eyes so you may see it, because, though few men ever know it, they do, my friend, they do.

McCANDLISH PHILLIPS

After silence, that which comes nearest to expressing the inexpressible is music.

ALDOUS HUXLEY

Praise is warming and desirable. But it is an earned thing. It has to be deserved, like a hug from a child.

PHYLLIS McGINLEY

The continual offering of praise requires stamina; we ought to praise God even when we do not feel like it. Praising him takes away the blues and restores us to normal.

HAROLD LINDSELL

Don't pat yourself on the back and boast and crow like a bloated rooster. People think you're a puffed up gas bag if you blow your own horn. Save your breath and your reputation. If praise is to be given, let it come from other people. Let them exalt and honor and say nice things about you if they're so inclined. Let them pour on the commendations and dish out the praise. It's amazing how far applause is heard if it's not the sound of a single hand clapping.

S. RICKLY CHRISTIAN

Praise is like a plow set to go deep into the soil of believers' hearts. It lets the glory of God into the details of daily living.

C. M. HANSON

We should be thankful for our tears; they prepare our eyes for a clearer vision of God.

WILLIAM A. WARD

There are three kinds of giving: grudge giving, duty giving, and thanksgiving.

ROBERT N. RODENMAYER

He who praises everybody, praises nobody.

SAMUEL JOHNSON

See also: Proverbs 27:2; John 12:43; Philippians 1:3; James 3:7–12

WEEK

11

THE BIRTHDAY REQUEST

> *What good will it be for a man if he gains the whole world, yet forfeits his soul?*

MATTHEW 16:26

It was a lavish birthday party fit for a king, complete with ice swans, music, neon lights, and fountains spouting pink champagne. And just when the everybody-who-is-anybody crowd was wondering if life could get any better, Salome took the stage in her sequined leotard with the plunging neckline clear down to here, and danced till King Herod's skin tingled. When she was done, the birthday boy whooped it up and told her to name her price—up to and including half his kingdom.

Since Salome was already a member of the royal brat pack and had everything a future teen queen could want, she asked her mother to make a wish. When she relayed her mother's message to the king, Salome leaned clear over, and her words were barely audible over the sound of Herod's pulse.

"I want you to give me right now the head of John the Baptist on a platter," she cooed, as eager as her mother to be rid of the Baptist party pooper who constantly harped about loose living.

As intoxicated as he was by Salome's eighty-proof perfume, Herod turned stone-cold sober when he heard her request. He was "greatly distressed," the Bible says, because he "knew [John] to be a righteous and holy man." He *knew* it. But in the end, "because of his oaths and his dinner guests, he did not want to refuse her." And so, figuring he had everything to gain and little of consequence to lose, he summoned the goon squad.

This tragedy, recounted in great detail by both Matthew and Mark, is one of the clearest pictures of the ultimate consequence of compromise. Aside from the fact that John lost his head in the deal, Herod was basically right in the short term. He won the approval of his party guests, and maybe even had a little fun with Salome on the side. In effect, he gained the world.

In the long run, however, he lost big. He lost his soul.

See also: Mark 6:17–25; Galatians 6:7

THE WHYS OF LIFE

> *The secret things belong to the Lord our God, but the things revealed belong to us and to our children forever, that we may follow all the words of this law.*
>
> **DEUTERONOMY 29:29**

Yesterday you read of the murder of John the Baptist, the man of whom Jesus once said, "Among those born of women there has not risen anyone greater" (Matthew 11:11).

I'm sure many people wondered why God allowed such a senseless tragedy to occur. After all, John wasn't just anybody. He was hand-picked by God to pave the way for Jesus' arrival. He was a good man, who didn't live high on the hog. He lived under the stars, ate bugs and honey, and wore a flea-bitten camel skin for clothing.

Questions regarding the whys of John's murder are met by silence in the Bible. There are no clues, no answers. What we do know is that Jesus didn't console his disciples by saying great good would come of John's death, or explain cheerily that they would someday understand God's purpose. He offered no platitudes like you hear these days. All the Bible says is that Jesus slipped away to mourn privately and pray.

Jesus, I believe, understood better than anyone else that sickness, pain, suffering, and death are realities of mortal life. He also understood clearly that nobody, himself included, was immune to it. If there was any big, ultimate purpose for John's life being snuffed out on a whim, I'm sure Jesus would have given a full, point-by-point explanation. But he didn't. He withdrew to be alone with God.

Because of the evil that exists in the world, we must all face and experience the hurts of life. But only for a little while longer. Soon now, very soon, there will be a new heaven and a new earth—without a trace of death or mourning or crying or pain. God will dwell among his people. Every tear will be wiped dry, and we will discover life as it was meant to be lived.

Until then, however, we must accept what we cannot change and content ourselves with knowing: "The secret things belong to the Lord our God, but the things revealed belong to us and to our children forever, that we may follow all the words of this law."

In other words, God has provided us a big enough peek into the goings-on of his universe to occupy us until he returns. The secret things, including answers to the *whys* of life, must be left to God.

See also: Acts 1:7; Revelation 21:4

THE UNTHINKABLE

I have chosen you and have not rejected you. So do not fear, for I am with you; do not be dismayed, for I am your God.

ISAIAH 41:9–10

Debbi considered herself to be a good Christian. She didn't smoke, swear, or do drugs. And she drank only occasionally. For nearly three years she'd dated Rob, a wonderful Christian boy. Though they had numerous opportunities to make love, Debbie and Rob chose to maintain their virginity. They were proud about their determination to remain pure, though they sometimes joked about being added to the endangered species list.

Midway through her senior year, the unthinkable happened. Debbi spent the night at a friend's house, got really drunk, and had sex with her friend's older brother. Almost immediately she knew she was pregnant, and her Hallmark world fell apart.

What could she do? An abortion, which she considered to be murder, was out of the question. And she'd probably get killed herself if she talked to her parents. As for Rob, if he found out their relationship would be over. The only way out, she figured, was to trap Rob into having sex so he'd think the baby was his. A quiet marriage could then be arranged.

But deep down, Debbi knew the solution she was toying with would end in disaster. King David was lesson enough. When he'd tried to hush up his shenanigans with Bathsheba by having her husband killed, he didn't get rid of his problem. He merely compounded it. And it wasn't long before he was a miserable, broken man. Sure, Rob could be seduced. He'd probably even marry her. But what would happen later, when he discovered he'd been duped?

In the end, Debbi risked everything and did what she knew was right. She came clean. It was the hardest, bravest thing she ever did, but she felt the Lord assuring her with the words from Isaiah 41:9–10: "I have ... not rejected you. So do not fear, for I am with you; do not be dismayed, for I am your God."

Though Rob called it quits, her friends and family rallied to help her through the crisis. And when Debbi's baby girl arrived, a loving Christian couple adopted her with open arms. Seeing their tears of joy didn't exactly make it all worthwhile, but they did help Debbi know she'd made the right decision.

When I think of Debbi, old-fashioned words like *intestinal fortitude*, and *guts*, and *strength of character* come to mind. Yes, she'd made a big, stupid mistake. But I think our mistakes, in God's eyes, are less important than our response to them. Debbi didn't run; she stood firm. And the Lord stood beside her. Together, they made quite a pair!

See also: 2 Samuel 11–12; Isaiah 40:28–31; Romans 8:31

LITTLE THINGS

Whatever is true, whatever is noble, whatever is right, whatever is pure, whatever is lovely, whatever is admirable—if anything is excellent or praiseworthy—think about such things.

PHILIPPIANS 4:8

In the Rodgers and Hammerstein musical "The Sound of Music," there's a catchy little song in which Maria, the lead character, sings of the wonder of raindrops on roses, whiskers on kittens, bright copper kettles, warm woolen mittens, and brown paper packages tied up with strings. "These," she sings, "are a few of my favorite things."

Though pumped full of NutraSweet, the song is a reminder to take pleasure in the little things. Unfortunately, we generally take such things for granted—all because we spend so much time worrying and grumbling and fretting and stewing and grousing and complaining about *equally* little things.

Chunks of entire days can be ruined because *"DAADDD!"* used your razor; somebody (*For the billionth time, Dorkface, I've gotta GO!*) is hogging the bathroom; somebody (*Mom, I TOLD you tonight was a big deal!*) forgot to pick up your blouse from the cleaners; somebody (*STUPID LADY DRIVERS!!*) is moving slow when you're in a stage-ten rush.

When we're not focusing on somebody else, we're often kicking ourselves unnecessarily for everything from missing an easy shot (*What a total jerk! I shoulda had it!*) to saying the wrong thing (*Try sounding intelligent for a change, Bimbo!*) to blowing an obvious exam question (*Such a DUMBO!*).

All too often we notice the minor problems, the glitches. We harbor petty grievances. Most of the annoyances are hardly worth

146

complaining about, yet dwelling on them has a cumulative negative effect. That's why the apostle Paul encourages us to dwell instead on the positives—on things that are true, noble, right, pure, lovely, admirable, excellent, and praiseworthy.

Positive thinking sometimes sounds a little sappy. But once you get the hang of it, it's really not a bad way to spend the day.

See also: Romans 12:2; Colossians 3:2; 1 Peter 4:7–8

WHAT IFS

We know that in all things God works for the good of those who love him, who have been called according to his purpose.

ROMANS 8:28

On any given day when the sun is sitting just right and my feet are propped up and there isn't anything too terribly important going on, I drift off into never-never land and ponder "What if ..." questions.

What if I'd not gone to college? What if I'd married somebody else? What if I'd accepted that job in Hollywood? What if I'd decided *not* to become a Christian?

"What if" questions concern what might have been—the path not taken. When faced with a fork in the road, you've got to decide which way to go. Right or left? And once you head one direction, the life that awaited you along the other quietly disappears. The big mystery is never knowing what the other fork would have brought. Had I gone another direction, would my life be totally different? Would I be rich and famous? Would I be happier?

And what about our mistakes—the forks we gleefully head down expecting Disneyland, only to find something resembling a bad dream? I've made what I mostly consider smart decisions. I've got my wife to show for one of them. But I've made a few of the other

147

kind along the way. Nevertheless, God has used those bad decisions in a positive way in my life. In all things God has worked for the good—even in the negatives. In *all* things.

In the verse above, God promises to do that. But it's conditional. That is, the promise is yours *if* you love him and are called according to his purpose. Today, at this very moment, can you say you truly love the Lord? As you're reading now, can you say you are exactly where God wants you to be?

God can't make your decisions for you. They are yours alone to make; the consequences, yours alone to live with. But once you've made the decision, he'll be at your side every step of the way.

See also: Genesis 50:15–20; Romans 8:31–32; Ephesians 2:10

QUIET TIMES

The Spirit helps us in our weakness. We do not know what we ought to pray, but the Spirit himself intercedes for us with groans that words cannot express. And he who searches our hearts knows the mind of the Spirit, because the Spirit intercedes for the saints in accordance with God's will.

ROMANS 8:26–27

In my lonely keep-to-myself times,
Hear my sighs, Lord,
For I am tired of going unnoticed and unloved.
In my fearful I've-been-hurt-before times,
Hear my anxiety, Lord,
For I'm scared to stick my neck out again.
In my grieving words-can't-express-the-hurt times,
Hear my tears, Lord,
For I don't know if I can face tomorrow.

In my angry leave-me-alone times,
Hear my grinding teeth, Lord,
For I'm so blasted mad I could scream!
In my worried knot-in-the-gut times,
Hear my wrinkled brow, Lord,
For I'm burdened today by yesterday and tomorrow.
In my hectic hit-and-run times,
Hear my pounding feet, Lord,
For I'm running late instead of running to you.
In my searching I-don't-understand times,
Hear my shrugging shoulders, Lord,
For I struggle with the whys and hows of life.
In my troubled I've-done-it-now times,
Hear my beating heart, Lord,
For I feel the weight of having failed—again.
In my anxious I-need-action-now times,
Hear my tension, Lord,
For I get tired of smashing into closed doors.

See also: Joshua 1:5; Psalm 23

POINTS TO PONDER: WORRY

Who of you by worrying can add a single hour to his life? Since you cannot do this very little thing, why do you worry about the rest?

Luke 12:25–26

We would worry less about what others think of us if we realized how seldom they do.

Ethel Barrett

If a care is too small to be turned into a prayer, it is too small to be made into a burden.

ANONYMOUS

There are two days in the week about which I never worry. Two carefree days, kept sacredly free from fear and apprehension. One of these days is yesterday—and the other is tomorrow.

ROBERT BURDETTE

The thinner the ice, the more anxious is everyone to see whether it will bear.

JOSH BILLINGS

It is distrust of God to be troubled about what is to come; impatience against God to be troubled with what is present; and anger at God to be troubled for what is past.

SIMON PATRICK

Small ills are the fountains of most of our groans. Men trip not on mountains, they stumble on stones.

CHINESE PROVERB

No man ever sank under the burden of the day. It is when tomorrow's burden is added to the burden of today that the weight is more than a man can bear. Never load yourself so. If you find yourself so loaded, at least remember this: it is your own doing, not God's. He begs you to leave the future to him, and mind the present.

GEORGE MACDONALD

Never trouble trouble till trouble troubles you.

ANONYMOUS

You can't change the past, but you can ruin a perfectly good present by worrying about the future.

ANONYMOUS

The first thing, when one is being worried as to whether one will have to have an operation or whether one is a literary failure, is to assume absolutely mercilessly that the worst is true, and to ask What then? If it turns out in the end that the worst is not true, so much the better: but for the meantime the question must be resolutely put out of mind. Otherwise your thoughts merely go round and round a wearisome circle, now hopeful, now despondent, then hopeful again—that way madness lies. Having settled then that the worst is true, one can proceed to consider the situation.

C. S. LEWIS

Worry is rust upon the blade.

HENRY WARD BEECHER

Borrow trouble for yourself, if that's your nature, but don't lend it to your neighbors.

RUDYARD KIPLING

Anxiety does not empty tomorrow of its sorrows, but only empties today of its strength.

CHARLES H. SPURGEON

There is nothing that wastes the body like worry, and one who has any faith in God should be ashamed to worry about anything whatsoever.

MAHATMA GANDHI

Ulcers are something you get from mountain-climbing over molehills.

ANONYMOUS

It ain't no use putting up your umbrella till it rains.

ALICE CALDWELL RICE

God never built a Christian strong enough to carry today's duties and tomorrow's anxieties piled on the top of them.

THEODORE LEDYARD CUYLER

Anxiety is the natural result when our hopes are centered in anything short of God and his will for us.

BILLY GRAHAM

Worry and trust cannot live in the same house. When worry is allowed to come in one door, trust walks out the other door; and worry stays until trust is invited in again, whereupon worry walks out.

ROBERT G. LETOURNEAU

Don't tell me that worry doesn't do any good. I know better. The things I worry about don't happen.

ANONYMOUS

See also: Psalm 37:7–11; 46:1; Luke 10:38–42; Revelation 3:8

WEEK

12

GRAYBAR HOTEL

Do not get drunk on wine, which leads to debauchery. Instead, be filled with the Spirit.

EPHESIANS 5:18

Jerry did not want to go to the Graybar Hotel, but that's where he ended up on his eighteenth birthday after being arrested for drunk driving. He tried to explain that he'd only had two beers, but the officer said drunk was drunk.

Jerry's stay at the Graybar Hotel began with a breath test, followed by the gathering of his possessions, including his billfold and watch. They also took his belt, just in case his thoughts turned suicidal. An arrest report was typed, he was given a booking number, and was then led to a holding tank with eight other people (including a male prostitute who kept winking at him). An officer pointed out the phone on the wall and told Jerry he could make one call. He swallowed hard, then called home. When his mother heard where he was, she wept.

After being fingerprinted and photographed, he was issued a mattress cover and cheap blanket, and then ushered to a dormitory cell with twenty-three other men, most of whom smelled like ripe gym clothes. Before the night was over, two cell mates propositioned him and another shoved him up against the wall and threatened to beat his brains out for having sat on his bed. Jerry didn't dare go to sleep.

Rest room facilities consisted of a bank of sinks and toilets on the wall, in full view of everybody, including passersby in the hall. Since Jerry was the newcomer, his bunk was nearest to the toilets.

As for food, breakfast was scrambled eggs and toast washed down with a cup of water. After eating, Jerry returned to his cell where he whiled away the hours on his bunk, keeping a wary eye on his cell mates.

Due to the banks being closed, Jerry's father was unable to raise bail, so Jerry's stay was extended to Monday. Consequently, he had plenty of time to think about how easily he could have avoided his stay at the Graybar. He could have said no when the six-pack was passed.

As bad as the Graybar Hotel was, Jerry could have had it worse. He might have been taken to another facility for drunks across town. It's known as the morgue.

See also: Romans 13:11-14; 1 Corinthians 6:19-20

EXCUSES, EXCUSES

Mary took about a pint of pure nard, an expensive perfume; she poured it on Jesus' feet and wiped his feet with her hair. And the house was filled with the fragrance of the perfume. But one of his disciples, Judas Iscariot, who was later to betray him, objected, "Why wasn't this perfume sold and the money given to the poor? It was worth a year's wages." He did not say this because he cared about the poor but because he was a thief; as keeper of the money bag, he used to help himself to what was put into it.

JOHN 12:3-6

As one of the Twelve, Judas Iscariot was like a brother to Christ. For about three years they traveled the dusty roads side by side, shared the same food, and slept together beneath the stars. Despite his Judean roots (the others were from Galilee), Judas was treated like one of the boys. He was even entrusted with the group's money bag, which was a big mistake because he began skimming from the kitty.

I'm sure he excused his wrong as being no big deal. After all, he'd left a good job to follow Christ and wasn't compensated for what he was worth to begin with. Not to mention the long hours and extra responsibility—that had to be worth *something*. And as treasurer, wasn't it really within his job description to determine how the money

155

was paid out? Call it stealing or embezzlement if you will; in his mind he was just getting what he was due.

The Bible is clear that the consequence of unconfessed sin is death. However, that doesn't happen overnight. Judas didn't suddenly palm a quarter from the cookie jar and then find himself in hell. It was a long gradual slope with a downward grade so slight that he probably didn't even notice it. But each time he excused or minimized his petty thievery, he took another step down that slippery path. For Judas, the path took a downward plunge when the money purloined from the cookie jar was no longer enough. Judas wanted more.

Judas eventually got what he wanted—a little side job with a tidy payoff. However, the side job happened to involve betraying the Son of God. Later, after he'd done his dirty work, he felt tremendous remorse. In fact, he got so worked up when he thought about the nice guy he used to be and the devil he'd become that he returned the money. And then he promptly went out and tied a noose around his neck.

He was sorry—all the way to hell.

See also: Matthew 26:14–16; 27:3–5; Romans 6:23

THE MONSTER

While [Christ] was still speaking, Judas, one of the Twelve, arrived. With him was a large crowd armed with swords and clubs, sent from the chief priests and the elders of the people. Now the betrayer had arranged a signal with them: "The one I kiss is the man; arrest him." Going at once to Jesus, Judas said, "Greetings, Rabbi!" and kissed him.

MATTHEW 26:47–49

I don't like to think too long about Judas because my mind always swells with disgust. What kind of man could share three solid years of both good and bad times—of holy, supernatural times—with Jesus, witness all of the miracles, hear all of the teaching ... and then betray him with a kiss of death? What was the traitor really like? How is it possible for a fellow human being to act as Judas acted? Was he a madman? A monster?

Those same questions were posed of Adolf Eichmann, a principal architect of the German Holocaust. The executioner of millions of Jews, Eichmann stood trial in 1961. People expected to see a cunning man full of malice and sadistic savagery. What they found, instead, was that evil doesn't always look monstrous.

This was most apparent when Yehiel Dinur, a concentration camp survivor, entered the courtroom to testify against Eichmann. As he strode down the aisle to mount the witness stand, he suddenly stopped and wheeled around to face Eichmann. The courtroom hushed silent. And then Dinur did something strange: he began to weep. Moments later, he crumpled unconscious to the floor.

Was Dinur overcome by hatred? Fear? Horrid memories? No, he was simply overcome to discover that evil looks like what you see when you look in the mirror. As he later told reporters, he realized all at once that Eichmann, who'd turned killing into a science, was not some animal, but just an ordinary human being. And in that moment of understanding, "I was afraid about myself," he said. "I saw that I am exactly like he."

The same can be said of Judas. Like Eichmann or any of our latter-day madmen, the man who betrayed Christ was *normal*. A more scary thought is hard to imagine.

See also: Isaiah 64:6; Romans 3:10–18, 23; 7:24

GROWING UP

Since you already know this, be on your guard so that you may not be carried away by the error of lawless men and fall from your secure position. But grow in the grace and knowledge of our Lord and Savior Jesus Christ.

2 PETER 3:17–18

If you've been a Christian for any length of time, it is easy to become comfortable in your relationship with Christ. You're on a first-name basis now, and things seem to be going fairly smoothly. The most obvious sins have already been dealt with, and the little nuisance sins that remain behind don't really seem all that harmful. So is it too much to ask that Christ just settle in, put his feet up and his tools away, and quit poking around?

The question, however, is not how comfortable you are with the relationship, but how comfortable Christ is in your heart. C. S. Lewis addressed this very topic in his book *Mere Christianity:*

Imagine yourself as a living house. God comes in to rebuild that house. At first, perhaps, you can understand what he is doing. He is getting the drains right and stopping the leaks in the roof and so on: you knew that those jobs needed doing and so you are not surprised.

But presently he starts knocking the house about in a way that hurts abominably and does not seem to make sense. What on earth is he up to? The explanation is that he is building quite a different house from the one you thought of—throwing out a new wing here, putting on an extra floor there, running up towers, making courtyards.

You thought you were going to be made into a decent little cottage: but he is building a palace. He intends to come and live in it himself.

See also: Ephesians 4:15; Philippians 2:12–13; Revelation 3:20

THE MOMENT OF TRUTH

*Consider him who endured such opposition from
sinful men, so that you will not grow weary and lose heart.
In your struggle against sin, you have not yet resisted to
the point of shedding your blood.*

HEBREWS 12:3–4

I considered her a casual friend, but she thought we were
an item made in heaven. When she pushed the relationship, however, I explained I didn't want to get serious; I just wanted to be
friends. That's when she started to cry.

Not knowing what to say or do, I put my arm around her and
told her not to cry. She didn't say anything for a while. But then she
finally looked up and, with a vulnerable but inviting tone in her
voice, said, "I'd do anything to stay close."

I looked at her to see if I was hearing her correctly.

"Anything?"

She blushed a little, and then nodded.

"You mean ..."

"My parents won't be home Saturday."

In the next several moments, a full-scale war broke out in
my heart as I toyed with temptation. I told myself the idea was
wrong, and then teased myself into believing it was really no big
deal. Who would know? Who would care? I halfheartedly asked
God's help to resist ... and then the moment of truth came, and I
had to say something.

Our eyes caught and I forced a smile. And then weakly,
grudgingly, I shook my head no. "God has something better for both
of us," I said quietly.

During subsequent weeks, I replayed the conversation over
and over in my mind. What I felt was not a sense of victory or virtue

159

for having withstood temptation, but a dull, worn-out, exhausted feeling. And in those tired moments, I was again reminded just how hard it is to live the Christian life, because if it's lived right, it's lived in direct opposition to Satan.

Of course, God never promised that the Christian life would be easy. It's warfare, pure and simple. And there are days when you can feel the battle clear to your bones.

See also: James 4:7; 1 Peter 2:11

BIG FIVE

For the grace of God that brings salvation has appeared to all men. It teaches us to say "No" to ungodliness and worldly passions, and to live self-controlled, upright and godly lives in this present age, while we wait for the blessed hope – the glorious appearing of our great God and Savior, Jesus Christ, who gave himself for us to redeem us from all wickedness and to purify for himself a people that are his very own, eager to do what is good.

TITUS 2:11–14

Sitting in the darkened room, team members stare at the flickering images on the screen before them. The movie, shot at the preceding week's game, is without sound. But the room is abuzz with conversation. Out of the darkness, the coach barks comments to the players, identifying weaknesses that can be attacked in the coming week's practices.

"Number 42, you gotta stay with your man! A little head fake, and he moved right past you ... You call that blocking? Come on, girls, gotta dig in and stay low ... Number 16, keep your eyes on the game, not the cheerleaders!"

Identifying specific problem areas can be valuable for us as Christians, too. To live victorious, faithful lives, it takes more than praying that God help us become better Christians.

Better in what areas? Getting better control of your tongue? Improving your thought life? Eating less? Kicking a certain bad habit? Mending a certain relationship?

Take a few minutes and jot down five specific areas you'd like to work on in the days ahead, using a short phrase or word:

The Big Five

1. _____
2. _____
3. _____
4. _____
5. _____

If you can't honestly say you are drawing closer to God, the Big Five is probably the reason why. Talk to God about helping you overcome these specific obstacles, and thereby shorten the list. And don't forget, it's not your problem exclusively. God has a lot at stake in the outcome. He's on your side, rooting for you to succeed.

See also: Ephesians 2:10; Philippians 2:12–13; 3:14

POINTS TO PONDER: TEMPTATION

When tempted, no one should say, "God is tempting me." For God cannot be tempted by evil, nor does he tempt anyone; but each one is tempted when, by his own evil desire, he is dragged away and enticed. Then, after desire has conceived, it gives birth to sin; and sin, when it is full-grown, gives birth to death.

JAMES 1:13–15

Most people want to be delivered from temptation but would like to keep in touch.

ROBERT ORBEN

Lord, often have I thought to myself, *I will sin but this one sin more, and then I will repent of it, and of all the rest of my sins together.* So foolish was I and ignorant. As if I should be more able to pay my debts when I owe more; or as if I should say, "I will wound my friend once again, and then I will lovingly shake hands with him." But what if my friend will not shake hands with me?

THOMAS FULLER

Change your thoughts and you change your world.

NORMAN VINCENT PEALE

It is much easier to suppress a first desire than to satisfy those that follow.

FRANÇOIS DE LA ROCHEFOUCAULD

The things that I can't have I want, and what I have
    seems second-rate;
The things I want to do I can't, and what I have to do I hate.

DON MARQUIS

Inflation hasn't affected the wages of sin. It's still death.

BUMPER STICKER

Temptation is Satan's opening wedge into a man's being. He does not want to stop there. If a man will obey demonic promptings to do evil, Satan will do worse with him by far than merely to tempt him.

MCCANDLISH PHILLIPS

God's plan made a hopeful beginning,
But man spoiled his chances by sinning.

We trust that the story will end in God's glory.
But, at present, the other side's winning.

ANONYMOUS

Only those who try to resist temptation know how strong it is. . . .
A man who gives in to temptation after five minutes simply does
not know what it would have been like an hour later. That is why
bad people, in one sense, know very little about badness. They
have lived a sheltered life by always giving in. We never find out
the strength of the evil impulse inside us until we try to fight it:
and Christ, because he was the only man who never yielded to
temptation, is also the only man who knows to the full what temptation means — the only complete realist.

C. S. LEWIS

Virtue consists, not in abstaining from vice, but in not desiring it.
GEORGE BERNARD SHAW

As the Sandwich-Islander believes that the strength and valor of
the enemy he kills passes into himself, so we gain the strength of
the temptations we resist.

RALPH WALDO EMERSON

I can resist anything except temptation.

OSCAR WILDE

It is easier to stay out than get out.

MARK TWAIN

Better to shun the bait than struggle in the snare.

JOHN DRYDEN

See also: Matthew 26:41; 1 Corinthians 10:13; Hebrews 2:14–18;
4:15

WEEK

13

BULL'S-EYE

All kinds of animals, birds, reptiles and creatures of the sea are being tamed and have been tamed by man, but no man can tame the tongue. It is a restless evil, full of deadly poison. With the tongue we praise our Lord and Father, and with it we curse men, who have been made in God's likeness. Out of the same mouth come praise and cursing. My brothers, this should not be.

JAMES 3:7–10

The words came out of my mouth like the blast of a shotgun. Released in a moment of anger, they were sharp and biting. I'd been hurt and wanted to maim in return.

I could tell I hit the target because my words brought immediate tears. It was a bull's-eye blast, and I turned away feeling good inside.

The good feeling, however, barely lasted ten minutes. After that I felt awful. I'd gone too far. Instead of turning the other cheek, I'd retaliated. Not only that, but I'd retaliated at a level grossly out of proportion to my own private hurt. I'd merely had my ego bruised. It was as if I'd been grazed by a BB. In return, I'd pulled the trigger of a double-barreled Winchester at point-blank range, leaving a gaping wound.

A few days later I went back and said I was sorry, that I didn't really mean what I'd said. But even as I mouthed the words, I felt "sorry" was so inadequate. If I didn't mean it, then why did I say it? *Why?* It was like I was trying to patch up a bloody mess with a Band-Aid.

I know that the person I hurt could, to this day, repeat verbatim what I said when I lashed out years ago. Terrible pain goes deep, and hers went clear to the bone. She was probably not much different from a young woman I once read about. Before committing suicide, she left a note that simply read, "They said ..."

The note was never finished. Something "they said" killed her.

See also: Matthew 5:21–24; 1 Peter 3:8–12

166

LOW (VERBAL) BLOWS

Everyone should be quick to listen, slow to speak and slow to become angry, for man's anger does not bring about the righteous life that God desires.

JAMES 1:19–20

Most of the troubles and heartache I've caused other people have been smoothed over with a "sorry." It works better than Bactine on minor hurts. If I say the wrong thing, I merely need to mutter an apology and everything will be all right.

However, as the incident mentioned yesterday helped me realize, things aren't always that simple. Contrary to the kid's rhyme about sticks and stones breaking bones but words never hurting, low verbal blows can cause lasting damage. And the wounds they inflict can't always be bandaged over with apologies.

Imagine if every snub were that serious. Imagine if every time you lashed out, laughed at another's expense, ignored a lonely person or stood by while somebody was taunted by others—you couldn't patch things up with a "sorry." And what if you were held permanently responsible for even "minor" slights?

In actuality, that's the way things are. We can minimize our wrongs, but God can't. In the end, "he will say to those on his left, 'Depart from me ... For I was hungry and you gave me nothing to eat, I was thirsty and you gave me nothing to drink, I was a stranger and you did not invite me in, I needed clothes and you did not clothe me, I was sick and in prison and you did not look after me.... Whatever you did not do for one of the least of these, you did not do for me'" (Matthew 25:41–43, 45). In other words, when we hurt other people, even *indirectly*, it's the same as hurting Christ *directly*.

I sometimes wish God could shrug off these little things and not be so literal about right and wrong. But sin is serious business with him—to the extent that he demanded a drastic solution. Somebody had to pay the consequences. In the end, Christ stepped forward—to be ridiculed, laughed at, beaten, and finally killed—*on my behalf.*

Knowing that my sin prompted such a sacrifice and that Christ feels the pain when I hurt others, I am trying to adopt a less belligerent, more benevolent attitude toward others. And when I do blow it, "sorry" may work some of the time, but the only lasting relief is repentance.

See also: Romans 12:17–21; 1 Thessalonians 5:15; James 1:26

MEASURING UP

Do not love the world or anything in the world. If anyone loves the world, the love of the Father is not in him. For everything in the world—the cravings of sinful man, the lust of his eyes and the boasting of what he has and does—comes not from the Father but from the world. The world and its desires pass away, but the man who does the will of God lives forever.

1 JOHN 2:15–17

I sometimes wondered what it would be like to play on the varsity football team. With just a few more muscles in the right places, I could have strutted through the locker halls like I owned them, smiled and flirted with the cheerleaders, listened to my name boom over the loudspeakers, and watched as people jumped and hollered when I scored a touchdown.

I sometimes wondered what it would be like to be confined to a wheelchair. With just a little different body position on any number of accidents and "close calls," I could have been crippled for life. I could have rolled through the locker halls and been stared at, learned to eat without use of my hands, taught myself to write and paint by using my mouth, and had a special license plate so I could park near the front door of any store.

I sometimes wondered what it would be like to live in the really nice part of town. With a lot more money, I could have worn all of the right clothes, invited kids over to swim in a backyard pool, driven a really fast car, eaten out for lunch instead of always bringing brown bags, and not counted pennies every time I wanted to turn around.

I sometimes wondered what it would be like to be dirt poor and live on the other side of the tracks. With a lot less money, I could have slept on something besides a mattress, never washed with hot water because it takes money to heat water, never taken an aspirin or used deodorant because it takes money for that, too, and quit school at fifteen because the nice kids from good homes would make fun of my clothes and my smell.

I sometimes wondered about the tremendous disparity in life between the haves and have nots, the rich and the poor, the healthy and the sickly, the beautiful and the ugly, the wise and the foolish. I just thank God that each of us, regardless of the world's standards, stands equal before God. And someday soon, very soon, we will all be asked to give an account for our lives.

The only thing that will matter then is how we measure up to God's standards.

See also: Ecclesiastes 2:14–15; Luke 14:13–23; James 2:1–13

AS THE WORLD TURNS

God "will give to each person according to what he has done." To those who by persistence in doing good seek glory, honor and immortality, he will give eternal life.

But for those who are self-seeking and who reject the truth and follow evil, there will be wrath and anger.

ROMANS 2:6–8

Every morning in our local paper, one of the TV reporters writes about what happened the previous day on the various soaps. If there were not hundreds of people who wanted that information, the reporter would write instead about beached whales, sewage spills, or other community concerns. But he doesn't; he outlines the worst programs Hollywood has ever created.

Below is his verbatim report for "As the World Turns," a show which reflects human nature more accurately than anybody cares to acknowledge:

Margo had Tom served with divorce papers after catching him in a clinch with Barbara. Meg kept mum that she saw Holden kissing Lily. Marsha told her lawyer, Jennings, that she, not Doug, had kidnapped Frannie and Kim. Steve was livid to learn that Tad had outbid Steve on several construction jobs. Feeling snubbed by Lucinda, Lily decided to remain at Emma's farm. Lucinda is plotting to reunite Sierra and Craig. Sierra agreed to help Craig find out the identity of the mystery woman, who Craig believes is Shannon.

There's no tremendously deep or theological point to be made from this, other than to point out that if you want a quick glimpse of the vast disparity between God's standards and the world's standards, all you need to do is flip on the TV some afternoon when you happen to be home.

But if you have the faintest doubt as to where it all leads and what happens to those who side with the world instead of God, you won't find it on TV or in the newspaper.

For that you need your Bible.

See also: Romans 6:23; 2 Timothy 3:1–9; 1 John 2:17

THE JUNGLE

Be self-controlled and alert. Your enemy the devil
prowls around like a roaring lion looking for someone to
devour. Resist him, standing firm in the faith.

1 PETER 5:8–9

The South American village had its good side of town and its bad side. The bad side was close to the jungle where the Beni River began to pick up a little speed. The good side occupied a section surrounding a modern hotel. I happened to stay on the good side, so I remember the village as both clean and friendly. In fact, by Bolivian standards it was paradise.

So I was surprised recently to read that that same sleepy town was the scene of a brutal ambush that took the lives of many innocent people. I had been there just a short time before, and it didn't seem possible that such a heinous crime could occur in such a nice locale. But paradise or not, there was one thing I was forgetting: The jungle was not that far away.

Call it the "jungle of the heart," if you will—it is never that far away. Remember that the next time somebody leaves you in the wake of their turbo-charged ambition; the next time you forget your bearings and lash out at somebody in anger; the next time you see somebody making fun of a severely handicapped person. The jungle is not that far away.

Remember that the next time somebody you greatly respect shatters every perception of what you thought a good Christian was like; the next time you take a good look at the dark side of your soul; the next time you see a blatant display of hypocrisy in your church. The jungle is not that far away.

Remember it, too, the next time you are at the mall and find yourself lusting after the world's standards; the next time you

171

think that to be truly successful you've got to have a high-paying job, a fast car, and a big house; the next time you take a good look in the mirror.

The jungle, my friend, is not that far away.

See also: Luke 12:15; James 4:4–10

SHIFTING SAND

Everyone who hears these words of mine and puts them into practice is like a wise man who built his house on the rock. The rain came down, the streams rose, and the winds blew and beat against that house; yet it did not fall, because it had its foundation on the rock. But everyone who hears these words of mine and does not put them into practice is like a foolish man who built his house on sand. The rain came down, the streams rose, and the winds blew and beat against that house, and it fell with a great crash.

MATTHEW 7:24–27

When the O'Malleys bought their dream home on the sands of Long Island's Westhampton Beach, there was a sprawling dune and glistening beach separating them from the Atlantic. But gale-force winds kicked up the surf, and before long they were looking down the barrel of nature's gun.

They lost the dune their first winter, and the beach disappeared beneath their feet soon after. Two years later their roof and top floor were blown away. Rebuilding was a joke. Before long, their steps were gone, the homes on both sides of them toppled, and water lapped at their foundation. It was just a matter of time before their home was reduced to driftwood.

Like the O'Malleys, the Alfords bought a sea-view home. Theirs was atop a 160-foot cliff in Bolinas, California, and on a clear day they could see San Francisco. But when storms brewed, the churning water carved out great chunks of the cliff. One day there was a deep-rooted tree in their backyard; the next day it was gone, along with a fifteen-foot slice of their yard. Soon there was nothing but air between their deck and the raging surf below.

Foolish as it is to build on sand, it must be dreadful to watch your property reduced to driftwood. That's what Jesus was getting at in the verses above, except that he wasn't talking about real estate.

He was talking about those for whom the Word of God merely goes in one ear and out the other; those who go to church often enough to be considered religious, but nothing they hear ever really soaks in. Before long, their lives are eroded and splintered by the concerns of the world.

If you find yourself in that category today, you need to start, I mean *really* start, taking your Christianity seriously. You need to get solid rock beneath you, and fast. The water is rising.

See also: Matthew 7:21; James 1:22–25

POINTS TO PONDER: OUR WORLD

My soul yearns for you in the night; in the morning my spirit longs for you. When your judgments come upon the earth, the people of the world learn righteousness. Though grace is shown to the wicked, they do not learn righteousness; even in a land of uprightness they go on doing evil and regard not the majesty of the LORD. O LORD, your hand is lifted high, but they do not see it. Let them see your zeal for your people and be put to shame; let the fire reserved for your enemies consume them.

ISAIAH 26:9–11

173

The world has a lot of glitter, but it doesn't have the glow.

BILL FRYE

It is five minutes to twelve on the clock of the world's history.

ADOLPH KELLER

The ship's place is in the sea, but God pity the ship when the sea gets into it. The Christian's place is in the world, but God pity the Christian if the world gets the best of him.

ANONYMOUS

I don't know if there are men on the moon, but if there are they must be using the earth as their lunatic asylum.

GEORGE BERNARD SHAW

The holiest moment of the church service is the moment when God's people—strengthened by preaching and sacrament—go out of the church door into the world.

ERNEST SOUTHCOTT

If Christians withdraw from society because of the bewildering nature of its problems, they will soon lose the right to be heard.

GARY R. COLLINS AND JAMES F. JEKEL

To deny the prevalence of pain in the world and the perennial popularity of evil. To abdicate responsibility for them by assuming that God will take care of them very nicely on his own.... To dismiss them or to encourage others to dismiss them by stressing the promise of pie in the sky.... To maintain your faith by refusing to face any nasty fact that threatens it. These are all ways of escaping reality through religion and should be denounced right along with such other modes of escape as liquor, drugs, TV, or any simplistic optimism such as communism, anticommunism, jingoism, rugged individualism, moralism, idealism, and so on, which assume that if everybody would only see it our way, evil would vanish and all would be sweetness and light.

FREDERICK BUECHNER

Some in one way, and some in others, we seem to touch and have communion with what is beyond the visible world.

F. H. BRADLEY

Great men are they who see that the spiritual is stronger than any material force.

RALPH WALDO EMERSON

The view we entertain of God will determine our view of the world.

CHRISTOPH ERNST LUTHARDT

The world is like a board with holes in it, and the square men have got into the round holes, and the round into the square.

GEORGE BERKELEY

Whoever marries the spirit of this age will find himself a widower in the next.

W. R. INGE

Secularism has this age by the throat.

WALTER LOWRIE

In this society we save whales, we save timber wolves and bald eagles and Coke bottles. Yet, everyone wanted me to throw away my baby.

VICTORIA, A PREGNANT WOMAN

The world hopes for the best but Jesus Christ offers the best hope.

JOHN WESLEY WHITE

O Lord, support us all the day long, until the shadows lengthen and the evening comes, and the busy world is hushed, and the fever of life is over, and our work is done. Then in Thy mercy grant us a safe lodging, and a holy rest, and peace at the last.

BOOK OF COMMON PRAYER

The world is charged with the grandeur of God.

GERARD MANLEY HOPKINS

What the soul is in the body, this the Christians are in the world. Christians hold the world together.

LETTER TO DIOGNETUS

See also: Matthew 5:13–16; Romans 6:23; James 4:4; 1 John 2:15–17

RUN THE RIVER

I will lead the blind by ways they have not known, along unfamiliar paths I will guide them; I will turn the darkness into light before them and make the rough places smooth. These are the things I will do; I will not forsake them.

ISAIAH 42:16

At the beginning, the water is calm, the paddling easy. You watch the terns fly above the canoe and take a few pictures of the towering gorge through which the river cuts. Suddenly you hear a distant roar—not unlike the rumbling of a sixty-car freight train. You swallow hard and grip your paddle until your knuckles turn white. The gorge narrows and the canoe sweeps faster. So does your adrenalin-charged blood.

Then, before you're ready for it, you're bouncing amidst haystack waves. Spray whips your face and four inches of water slosh in the canoe at your knees. "Pry on the left," your partner screams as a giant boulder looms directly in your path. But you only have time to shove off with your paddle.

Now the canoe is rocketing through a narrow chute. Aluminum canoes, bent like accordions, litter the banks and indicate what can happen if you get off course. You shudder but paddle furiously as the rapids kick and heave like a Brahma bull. Rocks scrape the bottom and bang the sides until . . . *WHOOOOMPHH!* . . . the current spits you headlong over the falls and into a quiet pool.

In many ways, life is like running a wild river in a canoe. It has its slow spells, its threatening spurts, its seat-of-the-pants thrills, its waterfalls, its tragedies. It keeps rushing by—sometimes at a roar, sometimes at a whisper—and if you're not careful you can get tossed around like a cork and go straight to the bottom. Or you can follow the guides and navigational charts and keep straight on course. You'll still go through the waterfalls and rapids, but you'll be on *top* of the water.

The only true guide, of course, is Jesus Christ. He's mastered the river; he knows it like the back of his hand. And he's left behind a helper and navigation maps for you. If you pay attention and study faithfully, you'll come out on top.

See also: John 14:26; 2 Timothy 3:16–17; Hebrews 12:1–3

TONGUE POWER

> *Pleasant words are a honeycomb, sweet to the soul and healing to the bones.*

PROVERBS 16:24

Congratulations.
The test is canceled.
I love you.
You've been accepted.
You look great.
Don't bother eating the vegetables.
I am sorry.
You are right.
The growth is benign.
You're on the team.
I forgive you.
You'll do better next time.
Stay out as long as you want.
Keep the change.
I'll write you.
Yes.
Happy birthday.
I'm praying for you.
You're hired.
There are seconds on dessert.

You have no cavities.
The car is yours.
Ball four.
Take a break.
You're right.
Get well.
You've done a good job.
Have a safe trip.
Sweet dreams.
My treat.
Let me help.
God bless you.

As Christian Nestell Bovee once said, "Kindness is a language the dumb can speak and the deaf can hear and understand."

See also: Proverbs 15:1–4; Philippians 4:8; Hebrews 3:13

REAL TEARS

I say to every one of you: Do not think of yourself more highly than you ought.

ROMANS 12:3

I thought prejudice was something you only read about in old newspapers and history books, something that happened back in the fifties in places like Alabama. After all, our school was a salad bowl of people of color—and everybody mixed well. Prejudice just didn't seem to exist.

Things changed when Samir started school in May, just before the summer break. At that time of year, the kids were looking for diversions to help get them through the last few weeks of school. Samir became that diversion. He was from Syria or Iran or someplace you only heard about on the evening news. It didn't really matter. What mattered was that he spoke broken English, dressed funny, and looked different.

A couple of the football players had a heyday with him, slipping drugs into his food when he wasn't looking. The next hour in class he was like a parakeet on speed, and nobody could shut him up. The teacher finally sent him to the office, but somebody steered him instead into the girl's locker room.

On another occasion, he was preparing a short speech about his country and sought help from students whom you wouldn't trust to walk your dog if you cared about your dog. As a joke, they peppered his script with four-letter words.When he gave the speech, everybody but Samir roared with laughter. He just stood there with a pained look on his face and then did something nobody had ever done before in English class. He began to cry.

All along people treated Samir like he was different. And difference led to prejudice. It was bigotry, pure and simple. But when they saw his tears, understanding began to sink in. You could see it on people's faces as they looked around at each other, and then looked down. He wasn't an animal, but a real live human being. They had sense enough to recognize that his hurt, his tears were no different from their own.

More important, they had sense enough to be ashamed.

See also: Psalm 131:1; Isaiah 5:21; Romans 12:16

ROUND TUIT

Obey what I command you today.

One Round Tuit
This is yours! Cut it out and keep it!

There is finally a sufficient quantity of these for all Christians to have their very own. Guard it with your life. Never lose it, and don't let anyone take it away from you.

These tuits have been hard to come by, especially the round version. But here are now enough to go around, and the timing couldn't be better because the demand has been overwhelming. At long last, many of your problems concerning your relationship with God and really getting down to serious, daily Bible study and prayer time will be solved. You can expect your attention span to double and your interest level to increase dramatically now that you have your own round tuit.

As you have often said, "I will start spending regular time alone with God once I get a round tuit." You have also commented, "I know I should read my Bible more, but I just haven't been able to get a round tuit."

Well, now that you've got it, use it!

See also: 1 Timothy 4:13–16; Hebrews 4:7; 6:11–12

BIG DREAMS

Jabez was more honorable than his brothers. His mother had named him Jabez, saying, "I gave birth to him in pain." Jabez cried out to the God of Israel, "Oh, that you would bless me and enlarge my territory! Let your hand be with me, and keep me from harm so that I will be free from pain." And God granted his request.

1 CHRONICLES 4:9–10

Compared to all the big-time, high-profile saints and scoundrels who show up in the Bible, Jabez is a small fry, a bit player. Placed side by side with the prophets, potentates, and assorted nabobs, he's a nobody.

Though his role in the Bible is limited to a paragraph buried amidst genealogy records in 1 Chronicles, it makes fascinating reading. It's a cameo appearance which you'd miss if you blinked at the wrong time.

All that's known about him is conveyed in the verses above. To rehash the facts, he acquired his funny name (which sounds like the Hebrew word for pain) because his birth practically did his mother in. Although he was a good, clean-living kid, he seems to have had a rough life—perhaps because other kids teased him about his name and gave him periodic black eyes.

But the day came when he decided enough was enough, and he asked God to help keep him safe and to give him bigger challenges—to "enlarge his territory."

That's about all the Bible has to say about Jabez, other than to report that God answered his prayer. Jabez wanted bigger challenges and more opportunity, and he got it.

I believe God is eager to do the same for any one of us, providing our ambition is not motivated by selfish desire. The problem is, we're often too content in our own little ruts. It's never crossed our minds to pray that God would enlarge our horizons. Or, to crib a thought from Jesus' brother James in the New Testament, "You wouldn't think of just asking God for it, would you?" (James 4:2 *The Message*).

See also: Psalm 37:4; Matthew 25:14–30; John 16:24; James 4:3

HEMMED IN

Make the most of every opportunity.

COLOSSIANS 4:5

If the characters in the Bible were thought of as movie actors and rated according to their prominence in the Scriptures, individuals

183

such as Jesus, Abraham, Moses, Paul, and David would get top billing. Their presence is felt throughout the Bible. Others such as Mary, Absalom, Goliath, Sarah, Herod, and Rahab would be cast in supporting roles.

Jabez, whom you read about yesterday, would be an "extra." He felt hemmed in by circumstances and people, and longed for bigger and better. But God heard his plea for broader horizons and, knowing his motives were honorable, gave him the desires of his heart.

Perhaps you know the claustrophobic feeling of being hemmed in by people and their attitudes toward you. To them you're a nobody because you don't turn heads in a swimsuit, can't slam-dunk a basketball, or won't play by their rules. Maybe others look down on you because of your age.

Or perhaps you feel hemmed in by circumstances; you know you are missing growth opportunities because you live on the wrong side of town, don't have the "right" contacts, or can't afford the "right" school.

One thing is certain, however. Despite what others say or circumstances allow, God has given you abilities and spiritual gifts that are being under-utilized. All you need is the opportunity....

For starters, ask God to help you make the most of every opportunity that now lies before you at home, school, church, or work—and in every area of your life, whether spiritual, emotional, social, or mental. Once you're sure you are being faithful within your present confines, then ask God to begin knocking down a few walls. Thankfully, he isn't bound by the barriers that surround us.

See also: 1 Corinthians 15:58; Philippians 2:1–3; 1 Timothy 4:12

POINTS TO PONDER: AMBITION AND SUCCESS

If anyone would come after me, he must deny himself and take up his cross daily and follow me. For who-

ever wants to save his life will lose it, but whoever loses his life for me will save it. What good is it for a man to gain the whole world, and yet lose or forfeit his very self?

LUKE 9:23–25

If you wish to reach the highest, begin at the lowest.

PUBLILIUS SYRUS

The true goal of the Christian life is heaven: nothing more, nothing less, and nothing else.

SHERWOOD ELIOT WIRT

An ambitious farmer, unhappy about the yield of his crops, heard of a highly recommended new seed corn. He bought some and produced a crop that was so abundant his astonished neighbors asked him to sell them a portion of the new seed. But the farmer, afraid that he would lose a profitable competitive advantage, refused. The second year the new seed did not produce as good a crop, and when the third-year crop was still worse it dawned upon the farmer that his prize corn was being pollinated by the inferior grade of corn from his neighbors' fields.

RALPH L. WOODS

Everybody wants to harvest, but nobody wants to plow.

ANONYMOUS

Some folks can look so busy doing nothin's that they seem indispensable.

KIN HUBBARD

He who dies with the most toys wins ... nothing. Luke 9:25.

BUMPER STICKER

God give me work till my life shall end, and life till my work is done.

WINIFRED HOLTBY

All you need in this life is ignorance and confidence, and then success is sure.

MARK TWAIN

It has always been my ambition to preach the gospel where Christ was not known.

THE APOSTLE PAUL, ROMANS 15:20

There are two tragedies in life. One is to not get your heart's desire. The other is to get it.

GEORGE BERNARD SHAW

A life spent in constant labor is a life wasted, save a person be such a fool as to regard a fulsome obituary notice as ample reward.

GEORGE JEAN NATHAN

Aim high. It is no harder on your gun to shoot the feathers off an eagle than to shoot the fur off a skunk.

TROY MOORE

Seek not the favor of the multitude; it is seldom got by honest and lawful means. But seek the testimony of the few; and number not voices, but weigh them.

IMMANUEL KANT

It seems to me we can never give up longing and wishing while we are thoroughly alive. There are certain things we feel to be beautiful and good, and we must hunger after them.

GEORGE ELIOT

If we make it our first goal always to please God, it solves many problems at once.

PHILIP E. HOWARD, JR.

Lack of something to feel important about is almost the greatest tragedy a person may have.

ARTHUR E. MORGAN

Nothing is too high for the daring of mortals; we storm heaven itself in our folly.

HORACE

Most people would succeed in small things if they were not troubled with great ambitions.

HENRY WADSWORTH LONGFELLOW

Not failure, but low aim, is crime.

JAMES RUSSELL LOWELL

To his dog, every man is Napoleon; hence the constant popularity of dogs.

ALDOUS HUXLEY

He is rich or poor according to what he is, not according to what he has.

HENRY WARD BEECHER

Success has always been a great liar.

NIETZSCHE

See also: Proverbs 3:5–6; Ecclesiastes 1:2–11; Luke 9:46–48; Philippians 2:3–11; James 3:13–18

WEEK

15

SEASONS OF LIFE

The body that is sown is perishable, it is raised imperishable; it is sown in dishonor, it is raised in glory; it is sown in weakness, it is raised in power; it is sown a natural body, it is raised a spiritual body.

1 CORINTHIANS 15:42–44

Every year about October, my favorite oak catches fire and the leaves explode like Fourth of July fireworks. It is a wondrous display of God's creativity: a flash of red up one branch, a burst of orange down another.

And then, quite suddenly, the leaves wither and dry. A couple of weeks later, the oak is bare and its black tree bones will stand like a skeleton through the long, cold winter until spring.

I can't think of that old weathered oak and its black tree bones without picturing some very special friends who are facing the winter of their lives. I think of Crystal, whose faith is as radiant as autumn leaves despite being trapped in a body withered by cerebral palsy. Despite the disease, she smiles bigger and sings praises louder than anybody I know. And not a day goes by when she doesn't roll her wheelchair into a corner to pray—for those less fortunate than her.

I also think of Harold, who met the Lord in prison while serving a double life sentence for crimes he didn't commit. He was eventually paroled and pardoned, but just when things were looking up he contracted throat cancer. To stay alive, he must now dilate his throat twice daily with an inch-thick, two-and-a-half foot long rubber tube. Despite his suffering, there's not a day he doesn't thank God for his tube, which enables him to keep breathing and to continue ministering to hurting people.

After the winter comes the spring, and every spring brings a miracle to my favorite tree. Its black tree bones, which seem so absolutely barren, suddenly burst with tiny green banners of life. It's an annual reminder that a similar miracle awaits me, my friends, and others who know Christ as Lord. Suffering and disease will be no more, our bodies will be transformed, our tears will be dried, and for the first time we'll discover life as it was meant to be lived.

Think of it like this. It will be as dramatic as watching new leaves erupt from old, withered, petrified tree stumps. It will be the Spring of springs. And on that day, that glorious, magnificent, long-awaited day, we'll finally stand face-to-face with our Lord, our Savior—the King of kings.

See also: 1 Corinthians 15:35–58; Revelation 21:2–4

RAMPAGE

> *We are therefore Christ's ambassadors, as though God were making his appeal through us.*
>
> 2 CORINTHIANS 5:20

Kevin came from a model family. The kids were very studious and, for the most part, great athletes. His two older brothers were basketball stars and went to college on athletic scholarships. Kevin wanted to follow in their footsteps. But, though he had their brains, the poor guy couldn't have hit a basket if it was hanging from his head.

It was a courtesy to the family that the coach let Kevin try out for the team. As expected, he didn't make it past the first cut. He had tears in his eyes when he headed out of the gym, which was understandable considering his dreams. At that moment, all he needed was for somebody to offer him an encouraging word, or maybe even a slap on the shoulder. Instead, one of the players tossed a grenade.

"Hey, Kevin, don't cry," he chided. "There's always the girls' team."

That afternoon, Kevin went on a rampage in his family's home, using a bat to smash windows, mirrors, lamps, appliances, and furniture. He then took his father's rifle and began shooting holes in the walls. By the time the cops got there, he'd done an estimated $30,000 in damage.

It was all pretty strange, especially since Kevin was the last guy you'd expect to go nutzoid. But it happened—in a nice neighborhood, to a good kid.

In actuality, however, Kevin's Dr. Jekyll/Mr. Hyde conversion is not isolated. Similar though less spectacular transformations occur every day. A cruel remark can force an insecure person into a neurotic shell. A biting put-down can deeply mar one's self-esteem. On the other hand, a kind word can give a person a boost he'll never forget, and loving encouragement can heal a multitude of hurts.

The amazing thing is that it's often within our power to decide which way the transformations will go. With a snub we can create horrors; with charity we can work miracles. It's a power that probably best belongs in the hands of God. But he has entrusted it to us as his representatives to the human race.

See also: 2 Corinthians 1:3–4; James 3:1–10

DESTINATION: HEAVEN

> *Since, then, you have been raised with Christ, set your hearts on things above, where Christ is seated at the right hand of God. Set your minds on things above, not on earthly things. For you died, and your life is now hidden with Christ in God. When Christ, who is your life, appears, then you also will appear with him in glory.*
>
> COLOSSIANS 3:1–4

As you read yesterday, you control an incredible power that can be used to change lives, whether for the positive or negative. That's what Christ was getting at when he said, "You are the light of the world" (Matthew 5:14). We're here to shine, to bring out the

God-colors in the world. In other words, we've been empowered with a serious and very sacred task: to help illuminate people's way toward heaven – out of their living hell. We are God's light-bearers.

As C. S. Lewis wrote, "It is a serious thing to live in a society of possible gods and goddesses, to remember that the dullest and most uninteresting person you talk to may one day be a creature which, if you saw it now, you would be strongly tempted to worship. Or else he may be a horror and corruption such as you now meet, if at all, only in a nightmare. All day long we are, in some degree, helping each other to one or the other of these destinations."

If you take the Bible seriously, everybody you know, every person you see at school or work, every member of your family, the president of the United States, the queen of England, the gas station attendant – *everybody* will one day arrive at one of two destinations: heaven or hell. Your role in their lives will help determine that eternal destiny.

Chances are, you don't run in the same circles as the president or the queen. But you do encounter dozens of other people who, by the light of Christ living in you, can be guided toward heaven. Before you do anything else today, think long and hard about the people you bump into who are not now heaven-bound. Pick the four you feel you can have the most influence on – and write their names below:

1. _____
2. _____
3. _____
4. _____

In the days and weeks ahead, pray daily for each of them. Ask God to soften their hearts toward the love and saving power of Jesus Christ and to convict them of their sins. More important, pray that God will empower you to help light up their lives ... and thereby help them toward heaven.

See also: Matthew 28:18–20; 1 Corinthians 10:31–33

IMAGINARY WORLD

He will command his angels concerning you to guard you in all your ways.

PSALM 91:11

The phone rang late at night, much later than people normally call. I knew I didn't want to hear whatever I was about to be told. As suspected, the news was tragic.

Vicky and Jim were returning from a fishing trip, and while driving along a mountain road they were blinded by the sun. For a split second, Jim wasn't sure where the road was—and then it was too late. The car went airborne, and they didn't have a chance.

Vicky and Jim were devout Christians whose young lives centered around their church. My natural inclination was to ask why God let such a senseless tragedy occur to them, of all people. After pondering this question, I tried to imagine a world in which bad things didn't happen to good people.

In such a world, I suppose the car would have sprouted a parachute and drifted to the valley floor. And what about other Christian friends I'd lost recently in an airplane crash? Couldn't God have gently lifted the plane so it cleared the mountain peak?

In that kind of imaginary world, everybody would want to have a Christian along for the ride ... just in case. Every airline would require a Christian on board, as would every ship. Buddy systems would be formed which paired Christians with others just to cross the street. Why risk injury or death when all you had to do was walk in the shadow of a Christian?

The scenario is ludicrous, of course. Yet the thought persists that somehow Christians receive a special dispensation from God which limits the extent to which they suffer. After all, doesn't the Bible clearly say God "will command his angels concerning you to guard you in all your ways"? Guard you from what? Sickness and death? No. Illness and death are intimate parts of the fallen world in which we live, and Christians are not immune from either.

Rather, his angels guard us from separation from God, which is the greater concern. For apart from God, we cannot say we have truly lived.

See also: Luke 9:25; Revelation 21:4

SUNSHINE SOLDIER

For I will yet praise him, my Savior and my God.

PSALM 43:5

It wasn't that Steve didn't believe in God. He did—provided God met his expectations and *acted like God*. That meant God would be a sort of celestial Daddy Warbucks and dole out health and happiness (plus an occasional bonus for good behavior) in lavish proportion at just the right moment.

For a while there, Steve was really quite the believer. He got good grades, even when he didn't crack a book the night before ("I prayed, and God just refreshed my mind!" he'd say); his acne was manageable ("A face made in heaven!"); he drove a fast car ("Praise God for freeways!"); and dated a girl who could have stopped a train with her looks ("After God made her, he threw away the mold!").

But then cracks developed in Steve's porcelain life that he wasn't able to patch over too well. In one six-month period, his father ran out on his mom, his train-stopping girlfriend took an interest in a member of the varsity swim team, and he jumped a curb in his car and crashed into a eucalyptus tree.

Suddenly God just wasn't acting much like God anymore. Or so it seemed to Steve. From his perspective, how much of a God could God really be if he couldn't solve Steve's problems? No God that Steve was interested in.

In the end, Steve's beliefs were entirely conditional: He'd go through the motions with God *if* God blessed him and kept things running smoothly. Unfortunately, life isn't always so smooth and neat. In some countries, becoming a Christian means nothing but heartache: you lose your job, get disowned by your family, and face jail or death. Not all Christians are born in Beverly Hills; some live in dumps.

In today's verse, the psalmist says, "I will *yet* praise him, my Savior and my God"—regardless of circumstances. God calls us to love him, no strings attached.

That's a tall order, but it's not one-sided. God made the same pledge to us and backed it with Jesus Christ.

See also: Deuteronomy 6:5; Psalm 44:22; Romans 5:6–8

IF ONLY …

This is how God showed his love among us: He sent his one and only Son into the world that we might live through him. This is love: not that we loved God, but that he loved us and sent his Son as an atoning sacrifice for our sins.

1 JOHN 4:9–10

Robin had heard all the talk about Jesus and how he'd supposedly vacated heaven and become a man. The whole idea seemed rather farfetched, and she just smiled every time her friends tried to raise the subject with her.

Then one winter night she was sitting home alone as it began to snow. The flakes seemed to float down at first, but the wind kicked up and the snow began falling like there'd be no tomorrow. As she was watching the storm from the warmth of the house, a bird suddenly flew smack into the plate-glass window in front of her and fell back into the snow. The *thump!* startled her, and she felt her heart racing. And then, just as suddenly, another bird hit the glass, followed by another and another.

Staring outside into the dark storm, Robin spotted a swirling flock of birds cutting against the wind and then pelting the window. She'd never seen anything like it before and couldn't figure it out. And then it struck her: caught in the violent storm, the birds were trying to seek shelter.

They'll all die out there! she thought as she grabbed her heavy jacket, pulled her gloves and boots on, and then ran outside. She made her way across to the big barn, threw open the door and turned on the floodlights. She waited expectantly, but the birds did not come inside. She jumped up and down, waving her hands in the doorway, but the birds ignored her.

As a last resort, she grabbed a broom and circled behind the house, trying to come at the birds from the opposite direction and shoo them into the protective shelter. But the birds did not understand.

If only I could become a bird, she thought. *Then I could lead them to safety and warmth; then I could save them—or at least communicate with them.*

Unable to do anything more, she gave up her lifesaving efforts and returned to the house, where she watched the birds continue slamming into the glass and dying in the cold.

If I could only become a bird! she thought again.

A sudden faraway look clouded her eyes, and for a moment it was not the birds she was thinking of, but Jesus. Maybe, just maybe, her friends were right.

See also: John 3:16; Romans 5:6–8; Philippians 2:5–11

POINTS TO PONDER: DOUBT AND UNBELIEF

The fool says in his heart, "There is no God."

PSALM 14:1

The difference between the unbelieving fool described by the psalmist and the "God is dead" theologian is that the Old Testament fool said in his heart there was no God; the modern fool brays it all over the countryside.

MARTIN P. DAVIS

Whether your faith is that there is a God or that there is not a God, if you don't have any doubts you are either kidding yourself or asleep. Doubts are the ants in the pants of faith. They keep it awake and moving.

FREDERICK BUECHNER

Men talk of "finding God," but no wonder it is difficult; He is hidden in that darkest hiding-place, your heart.

CHRISTOPHER MORLEY

It takes more credulity to accept the atheistic position than most men can muster.

GERALD KENNEDY

Doubt is a pain too lonely to know that faith is his twin brother.

KAHLIL GIBRAN

To be a true atheist is to acknowledge no rule except the rule of thumb.

FREDERICK BUECHNER

An atheist does not find God for the same reason a thief does not find a policeman. He is not looking for him.

WENDELL BAXTER

Two men please God—who serves Him with all his heart because he knows Him; who seeks Him with all his heart because he knows Him not.

NIKITA IVANOVICH PANIN

An atheist is a man who has no invisible means of support.

FULTON J. SHEEN

Doubt makes the mountain which faith can move.

ANONYMOUS

A little philosophy inclineth men's minds to atheism; but depth in philosophy bringeth men's minds about to religion.

FRANCIS BACON

Nobody talks so constantly about God as those who insist that there is no God.

HEYWOOD BROUN

There are no atheists in the foxholes of Bataan.

DOUGLAS MACARTHUR

In all affairs it's a healthy thing now and then to hang a question mark on the things you have long taken for granted.

BERTRAND RUSSELL

An agnostic is somebody who doesn't know for sure whether there really is a God. That is some people all of the time and all people some of the time.

FREDERICK BUECHNER

Few men are so obstinate in their atheism that a pressing danger will not compel them to the acknowledgment of a divine power.

PLATO

Every effort to prove there is no God is in itself an effort to reach for God.

CHARLES EDWARD LOCKE

Sartre speaks of the silence of God, Heidegger of the absence of God, Jaspers of the concealment of God, Bultmann of the hidden-ness of God, Buber of the eclipse of God, Tillich of the nonbeing of God, Altizer of the death of God. And the New Testament? It speaks of the love of God.

RICHARD WOLFF

Many an atheist is a believer without knowing it just as many a believer is an atheist without knowing it. You can sincerely believe there is no God and live as though there is. You can sincerely believe there is a God and live as though there isn't.

FREDERICK BUECHNER

Skepticism is a slow suicide.

RALPH WALDO EMERSON

If there is a God, atheism must seem to Him as less of an insult than religion.

GONCOURT

I think the trouble with me is lack of faith. I have no rational ground for going back on the arguments that convinced me of God's existence: but the irrational deadweight of my old skeptical habits, and the spirit of this age, and the cares of the day, steal away all my lively feeling of the truth, and often when I pray I wonder if I am not posting letters to a non-existent address. Mind you I don't think so—the whole of my reasonable mind is con-vinced: but I often feel so. However, there is nothing to do but to peg away. One falls so often that it hardly seems worth while picking oneself up and going through the farce of starting over again as if you could ever hope to walk. Still, this seeming absurdity is the only sensible thing I do, so I must continue it.

C. S. LEWIS

See also: Matthew 14:22–31; Mark 9:17–24; John 20:24–29

A LOVE STORY

He is the image of the invisible God.

COLOSSIANS 1:15

In a dark corner of my garage, tucked inside a grocery bag and sealed within a cardboard box, are untold dozens of letters I exchanged with the girl whom I eventually married. Not all are love letters. Quite a few are hesitant get-to-know-you letters which were signed, *Sincerely, Rick.*

We didn't fall in love the usual way. While I was in England studying and traveling for a year, a girl named Julie sent me a letter. I sent one back, and she wrote another. Before long we were writing every week. She'd tell me about her life and send me little things like pressed flowers, and I'd relay my escapades half a world away.

After about the twenty-fifth letter, my *Sincerely, Rick* had changed to *Love, Rick,* and I didn't want to write another word. For all I knew, the girl weighed three hundred pounds and didn't shave. But I was in love and wanted to hop the next plane home to check her out. I'd carried the relationship about as far as possible by mail; to go any further, I needed to *see* her.

People in past centuries felt the same frustration in their dealings with God. He maintained a strictly long-distance relationship, and nobody could really get close. Nobody ever got to *see* him.

Then something amazing and totally radical happened. God became visible. It wasn't a case of *Presto! Change-o!* where he was here one moment, gone the next. He lived on earth for thirty years, mingling with people and developing personal, face-to-face relationships. The world has never been the same since.

It is, truly, the world's greatest love story. A story not only told and written about, but the greatest ever *seen.*

See also: John 1:18; Ephesians 2:4–5; 1 John 1:1–3

THE UNVEILING

> *When John heard in prison what Christ was doing, he sent his disciples to ask him, "Are you the one who was to come, or should we expect someone else?"*

> MATTHEW 11:2–3

As if to prepare for his grand appearance on Planet Earth, which you read about yesterday, God arranged various sneak previews over several thousand years.

Early on, he appeared incognito—as an angel to Jacob, for example. But it was like trying to recognize somebody in a Halloween costume, and Jacob wouldn't have known who it was had not God finally just told him.

Later, with Moses, God used the disguise of a dust cloud and burning bush. Moses didn't mind the special effects and spoke with God "as a man speaks with his friend," but he eventually asked God to unveil himself. Even then, God only let him see his back, not his face.

It may have appeared that God had a case of stage fright and wouldn't come out of the dressing room. But I believe he was warming people up for the time he would put himself on public display; for the time people could walk right up and talk to him, or ask him any kind of stump-God question they could think of.

When that moment came, however, most people still didn't recognize him. One of Jesus' favorite questions to ask his disciples was, "Who do people say that I am?" I suspect he roared to hear some of their answers.

People were so mixed up that some thought John the Baptist was Christ and Christ was John the Baptist. Poor Johnny B.—who was supposed to "Make straight the way for the Lord"—was as befuddled as anybody and wasn't sure who he was fronting for.

Through go-betweens, he finally just asked: "Are you the one who was to come, or should we expect someone else?"

You'd think the religious leaders would have had some inkling as to who Jesus was, but they charged him with capital crimes *against* God. And when he was on trial for his life and needed all the friends he could get, his own disciples scattered.

Still, a few did recognize him. And to them God gave the right to be his body—through which he could reveal himself and continue providing glimpses of heaven on earth.

See also: Genesis 32:22–32; Exodus 3:1–6; 33:12–23

RUNAWAY

The son said to him, "Father, I have sinned against heaven and against you. I am no longer worthy to be called your son." But the father said to his servants, "Quick! Bring the best robe and put it on him. Put a ring on his finger and sandals on his feet. Bring the fattened calf and kill it. Let's have a feast and celebrate. For this son of mine was dead and is alive again; he was lost and is found."

LUKE 15:21–24

As far back as Danny could remember, he'd been prepped to follow in his father's footsteps and take over the family's insurance business. But at seventeen he was tired of the china-and-crystal lifestyle he'd grown up with, so he cashed in the savings bonds his parents had given him and, "over his father's dead body," hopped a train for Hollywood.

Though he stayed in a dingy motel and ate only once a day at the corner greasy spoon, Danny's money was gone in four months. A couple of young thugs he'd met on the street offered him a corner in their living room along with a candy jar of drugs, and the next two weeks were a constant high. Then they got him making cocaine drops, which seemed like no big deal until his "friends" accused him of skimming money, beat the bejeebers out of him, and left him bleeding in the gutter.

When the train whistles finally quit blasting in Danny's head, he wandered around an area of Tinseltown crowded with neon Budweiser signs and blinking marquees of raunchy theaters. He asked about getting work at the bars and strip joints—anything to make a little money. But one look at his split lip and broken nose, and he was shooed away.

Without a dime to his name, Danny finally did the only thing he could think of. He called home—collect. His father, over-joyed to hear his voice, promptly wired him money. The next morn-ing when Danny stepped off the plane in his dirty, blood-stained clothes, his father was there at the gate with open arms and tears in his eyes. Danny walked into his father's embrace, and for the first time in a very long time felt safe and warm and loved.

"We thought you were lost . . . forever," his father said, his tears brimming over.

"I thought I was lost, too," Danny finally said. "I've made a fool out of myself and have blown everything. But I'm home now if you'll take me; if you'll forgive me."

His father flashed a million-watt smile and, in a voice that seemed to come straight from heaven, said, "The family is wait-ing, son. Welcome home."

See also: Isaiah 1:18; Matthew 6:14–15; 1 John 1:8–9

TUG-OF-WAR

My Presence will go with you, and I will give you rest.
EXODUS 33:14

There are times when, looking back, I'd give anything for the chance to relive my high school years . . . but with the benefit of hindsight. That's not possible, I know. To paraphrase Longfellow, high school comes but once in a lifetime.

For me, high school was runaway hormones, acne, secret notes, student council, smelly gym socks, swimming pools, acne, a late-model Chevy, tennis courts, minimum-wage jobs, acne, and first loves. Did I say anything about acne? It was the absolute best, absolute worst, absolute most confusing of times.

A large part of my confusion had to do with figuring out who I was. If you asked people who knew me, they'd have said I was almost perfect. I was the student body president, newspaper editor, and letterman in tennis and swimming. I got mostly A's, had decent looks, came from a good home, and got along with most of my teachers. I suppose I was the person that others wanted to be. But I didn't want to be me.

I was tired of the words "responsibility" and "opportunity." All I wanted was the chance to be a normal kid who got into trouble just often enough to have fun. I wanted to take a break from being a leader and follow for a while. So I started doing things I normally wouldn't have done but thought I should do to fit in. For starters, I discovered what a hangover was.

However, I didn't enjoy waking up with train whistles blowing in my head or not being able to look myself square in the eye in the mirror. And I didn't enjoy the confusion of trying to be Mr. America on school days and Mr. Party Hearty on weekends. I felt torn in two, as though I was the object of a massive tug-of-war and the ref had just yelled, "Pull!"

About that time I met Becky. She was a leader type, but she knew how to have fun—without the headaches. Most of all, she had a sense of peace about her that I didn't share. One day she invited me to a Christian youth rally and there I discovered the source of her peace: the Prince of Peace. And I heard his two-thousand-year-old beckon, which changed my life: "Come to me, all you who are weary and burdened, and I will give you rest" (Matthew 11:28).

It was an outrageous, audacious claim. Yet all these years later, those words have the same power as when they were first spoken. "Come to me."

Are you listening?

See also: Joshua 24:15; Isaiah 40:28–31; Revelation 3:20

EXPERIENCED ONLY

"Not by might nor by power, but by my Spirit," says the Lord Almighty.

ZECHARIAH 4:6

Looking for a job, Rebecca opened the Sunday paper and flipped through the want ads. The little boxes shouted at her: *Experienced Only!* Even entry-level jobs seemed to require a Ph.D. or five years of prior experience.

Sometimes it may seem like the world is conspiring against you. Everywhere you turn, you are not old enough, smart enough, talented enough, experienced enough. At a time when you feel very adult and deal regularly with adult-sized concerns, you are constantly belittled and reminded of your youth.

It may help to know that some of the biggest biblical big shots faced similar struggles. Take Timothy, for example. A very close friend of Paul's, he was young enough that the apostle called him son and others ridiculed him about his age. Paul tried to console him by writing, "Don't let anyone look down on you because you are young, but set an example for the believers in speech, in life, in love, in faith and in purity." In other words, *physical* maturity matters less than *spiritual* maturity ... regardless of the world's standards.

That's the same message conveyed in the verses above to Zerubbabel. He was a bit player compared to leading man King Solomon. But God seems to enjoy apparent mismatches, and chose the young, ninety-eight-pound weakling to rebuild his temple. To ease Zerubbabel's feelings of insecurity, the Lord assured him that he was not working alone. The job would get done, he said, "Not by might nor by power, but by my Spirit."

In another instance, Jeremiah complained he wasn't old enough to do what God had in mind for him. But he was promptly reminded by the Lord, "Do not say, 'I am only a child.' . . . for I am with you."

Then as now, God can use your life in extraordinary ways if you trust him in very ordinary ways. Forget about age and talent and limitations. Put aside your feelings of insecurity and inexperience.

The Lord has big-time plans for those who care about their stature in God's eyes more than their appearance in man's eyes.

See also: Jeremiah 1:4–10; 1 Timothy 4:12

MEMORY CHALLENGE

I have hidden your word in my heart that I might not sin against you.

PSALM 119:11

As you read yesterday, our limitations are not liabilities to God. He recruits the young and inexperienced. There is no handicap that hinders our Lord.

No passage in Scripture explains that as well as the verses below, written by Paul. Read them over and over. And if you are up to a big challenge, commit the passage to memory.

It might help to know that actors memorize dozens of pages for a single stage performance. And some people have memorized entire books of the Bible. Even if you can't remember your social security number and struggle to recall your parents' birthdays, work at the following passage. It will take some time to get it down. But just what are you doing this week that's more important?

Take a good look, friends, at who you were when you got called into this life. I don't see many of "the brightest and the best" among you, not many influential, not many from high-society families. Isn't it obvious that God deliberately chose men and women that the culture overlooks and exploits and abuses, chose these "nobodies" to expose the hollow pretensions of the "somebodies"? That makes it quite clear that none of you can get by with blowing your own horn before God. Everything that we have—right thinking and right living, a clean slate and a fresh start—comes from God by way of Jesus Christ. That's why we have the saying, "If you're going to blow a horn, blow a trumpet for God" (1 Corinthians 1:26-31 The Message)

See also: Deuteronomy 6:6-9; Luke 18:27; James 2:1-9

POINTS TO PONDER: YOUTH

Remember your Creator in the days of your youth, before the days of trouble come and the years approach when you will say, "I find no pleasure in them."

ECCLESIASTES 12:1

Youth is preeminently the forming, fixing period, the spring season of disposition and habit; and it is during this season, more than any other, that the character assumes its permanent shape and color, and the young are wont to take their course for time and for eternity.

JOEL HAWES

The first sign of maturity is the discovery that the volume knob also turns to the left.

"SMILE" ZINGERS, CHICAGO TRIBUNE

Almost everything that is great has been done by youth.

BENJAMIN DISRAELI

Young people will respond if the challenge is tough enough and hard enough. Youth wants a master and a controller. Young people were built for God, and without God as the center of their lives they become frustrated and confused, desperately grasping for and searching for security.

BILLY GRAHAM

The sins of youth are paid for in old age.

LATIN PROVERB

The youth of a nation are the trustees of posterity.

BENJAMIN DISRAELI

Youth is the first victim of war; the first fruit of peace. It takes twenty years or more of peace to make a man; it takes only twenty seconds of war to destroy him.

BAUDOUIN I

A youth becomes an adult when he realizes he has a right not only to be right but also to be wrong.

THOMAS SZASZ

I, for one, hope that youth will again revolt and again demoralize the deadweight of conformity that now lies upon us.

HOWARD MUMFORD JONES

Experience is a wonderful thing; it enables you to recognize a mistake every time you repeat it.

ASSOCIATED PRESS NEWS SERVICE

For God's sake, give me the young man who has brains enough to make a fool of himself.

ROBERT LOUIS STEVENSON

It is better to be a young june bug than an old bird of paradise.

MARK TWAIN

There is a feeling of eternity in youth.

WILLIAM HAZLITT

It is not possible for civilization to flow backwards while there is youth in the world.

HELEN KELLER

At almost every step in life we meet with young men from whom we anticipate wonderful things, but of whom, after careful inquiry, we never hear another word. Like certain chintzes, calicoes, and ginghams, they show finely on their first newness, but cannot stand the sun and rain, and assume a very sober aspect after washingday.

NATHANIEL HAWTHORNE

Youth comes but once in a lifetime.

HENRY WADSWORTH LONGFELLOW

See also: Psalm 25:7; Ecclesiastes 11:9; 1 Timothy 4:12

WEEK

17

PERSONAL DELIVERY

In the beginning was the Word, and the Word was with God, and the Word was God. He was with God in the beginning. Through him all things were made; without him nothing was made that has been made....The Word became flesh and lived for a while among us. We have seen his glory, the glory of the one and only Son, who came from the Father, full of grace and truth.

JOHN 1:1–3, 14

I once worked for a company headed by a man who liked his privacy. As the founder, he didn't mingle with the employees, chat in the cafeteria, or wander the hallways. He remained secluded in his office behind closed doors.

When I was first hired, I was told by a couple of other employees that the founder didn't really exist.

"The silhouette you see through his lighted office at night is just a dummy, a mannequin." I knew they were putting me on, of course. I'd received a "welcome aboard" memo from him upon my hiring. But they shrugged it off.

"Dorothy thought the Wizard of Oz was real, too," they said.

Finally, three weeks after joining the company, I met the man face-to-face. I even shook his hand. The occasion? He had something important to tell me that he wanted to convey personally. What he had to say required my immediate attention. So we sat in my office talking for quite some time.

God, too, was something of a mystery. As you might expect of the world's founder, he more or less kept to himself. As you also might expect, many people doubted his existence because he seldom showed his face. He didn't mingle like one of the boys.

But then one day he threw the doors of heaven open wide and visited Planet Earth. Once and for all, the sound barrier was broken as the Word—the sum of all that God wanted to communicate—became flesh.

What he had to say could only be conveyed personally, and he did so in the person of Jesus. Just as God spoke creation into existence in Genesis 1, Jesus spoke salvation into existence. Forgiveness and freedom, judgment and joy, grace and love—it all became real. During his time on earth, he communicated his salvation message through leisurely conversation, intimate personal relationships, and, ultimately, his sacrificial death.

We don't casually walk away from his words. They require our personal attention. Our response to his message marks the difference between life and death.

See also: Galatians 4:4–5; 1 Timothy 3:16; Hebrews 2:14–15

BIT PLAYERS

The race is not to the swift or the battle to the strong.

ECCLESIASTES 9:11

When I go to the movie theater, I am generally one of the last out the door. The clean-up crews are already scraping gum, swabbing spilled Cokes, and sweeping popcorn off the floors as I sit and watch the last of the credits roll across the screen.

For most people, the movie ends when the couple kiss and walk off together into the sunset. But for me it's not over until I've seen the bit players credited: the "Screaming Lady" whose only line was a shriek when "Hoodlum #3" stole her purse, or the "Postman" whose five-second role consisted of being treed by a dog.

By staying until the projector shuts off, I make a social statement that is so subtle I am probably the only one who realizes I am making a social statement. Nevertheless, it's my way of saying there's no such thing as bit players—*everybody* is important.

That's the opposite of the world's view. The way you generally hear and see things, the only people who really matter are those with all of the looks and abilities, those who win gold medals and get elected, those who have large bank accounts and can remember punch lines. As for the rest, well . . . they are relegated to the background.

Every opportunity he got, Jesus thumbed his nose at those standards. You can see that in who he picked as his inner circle: not men who'd earned advanced theological degrees, but backwater lugs who could gut fish in three seconds flat. He kept his distance from the white-collar crowd, preferring instead the company of drunks, cheats, and assorted lowlifes.

When Christ wanted to demonstrate the power of God he healed the street-corner bum, and when he wanted to illustrate the grace of God he forgave the woman who'd warmed the bed of someone other than her husband. The poor, the meek, the runny-nosed kids—theirs is the kingdom of God, Christ said. As for those with Swiss bank accounts and MBA's from Harvard, they stand as much chance of making it through the pearly gates as a double-humped camel does of passing through the eye of a needle.

In the end, bit players received star treatment from Christ. And he challenges us to follow his lead by feeding the hungry, giving water to the thirsty and clothes to the poor, befriending strangers, nursing the sick, and even visiting the imprisoned.

It's not really a choice, but a command. And the extent to which you obey probably says more about you and your Christianity than anything else.

See also: Matthew 5:3–10; 19:13–14, 24; 25:31–46

LACK OF TRUST

Do not lie. Do not deceive one another.

LEVITICUS 19:11

Terri was a good friend through high school, but the relationship never held much promise because I never knew exactly how much I could trust her. All too often I caught her lying through her teeth.

Hers were not big, black, soap-opera lies, but little white ones—spread lavishly around whenever she needed to smooth things over or get out of a squeeze.

When a guy she didn't care about asked her out, she concocted some explanation about her parents having grounded her or long-lost relatives flying in to visit that particular night. If he phoned her at home, she stepped outside for a moment . . . and had her kid sister say she wasn't home. It was better to fib a little than crush a guy's ego, she reasoned.

What she didn't realize was that it hurt the guy more to be strung along with lame excuses than simply to be told from the outset she wasn't interested. The naked truth always hurts less than a lie in fancy clothes. But she never learned that.

When she blew an exam, Terri thought nothing of telling the teacher her grandmother had died and asking her to disregard the grade. Or when she was pulled over for speeding, she told the cop without flinching that her same grandmother was in an accident, and asked for a police escort to the hospital.

In a nutshell, truth wasn't an absolute standard for Terri, but more of an adjustable justification she used when convenient. As such, her word was worth about as much as a used movie ticket.

Ultimately, she developed a reputation for being superficial and insincere, and I always found myself second-guessing her. When she gushed praise, I questioned her motives. When she expressed absolute certainty about something, I figured she was merely trying to convince herself.

The sad thing about Terri was that she thought her white lies hurt nobody. But they did. And they hurt one person more than anybody else: Terri. She lost her integrity over these little matters, and her reputation never quite recovered.

See also: John 1:17; Ephesians 4:25

WEEDS OF DECEIT

Lord, who may dwell in your sanctuary? Who may live on your holy hill? He whose walk is blameless and who does what is righteous, who speaks the truth from his heart.

PSALM 15:1–2

The first recorded sin in the New Testament church was a lie (Acts 5:1–11). It happened when a man named Ananias sold a piece of property and, with his wife's full knowledge, pocketed some of the proceeds for a rainy day. The rest he donated to the church.

So far, so good. The problem is, he bragged around that he'd given the whole wad to charity.

When it came to matters of the heart, the apostle Peter was more sensitive than a lie detector. And as a former fisherman, he could smell a fish story a mile away. Something about Ananias's tale of largesse didn't ring true, so he eyeballed the church chiseler, told him he had not lied to man but to God, and then stepped back as Ananias dropped dead at his feet.

The second recorded sin was also a lie, courtesy of Ananias's wife, Sapphira. She showed up at church about three hours later, unaware she was a widow. Peter asked whether the amount Ananias donated represented the full proceeds of their real estate deal.

"Yes," Sapphira said, without batting an eye, "that is the price."

It was, of course, the couple's prerogative to hold money back. Since the property was theirs, they could have banked all of the proceeds and taken early retirement. They chose instead to give a big chunk of it to the poor box, and tell an even bigger lie. That was their mistake: they were pious frauds. And if the newborn Christian church was to prosper and grow, the weeds of deceit had to be pulled. Peter went right for the root.

"How could you agree to test the Spirit of the Lord?" he asked. "Look! The feet of the men who buried your husband are at the door, and they will carry you out also." And then Peter again took a step back as Sapphira, like her deceased mate, did a face plant at his feet.

"Lying to God is like sawing the branch you're sitting on," Frederick Buechner has written. "The better you do it, the harder you fall."

See also: Joshua 7:16–26; Psalm 73:27

MATTERS OF CONSCIENCE

Do not lie to each other, since you have taken off your old self with its practices and have put on the new self, which is being renewed in knowledge in the image of its Creator.

COLOSSIANS 3:9–10

As you might expect, the young Christian community in Jerusalem was scared stiff by the sudden deaths of Ananias and Sapphira, whom you read about yesterday. As Luke tells it in Acts 5, "Great fear seized the whole church and all who heard about these events." A few verses later he adds, "No one else dared join them, even though they were highly regarded by the people." That is, nobody would go near the church for fear God would get literal about the wages of sin being death.

I suppose there would be a lot fewer people in church today if God punished sin by triggering an occasional heart attack in the

221

middle of the service. Imagine if every now and then your pastor asked people to raise their hands if they'd cheated on their income tax or slept around outside of marriage. And imagine if those people who didn't raise their hands, but should have, suddenly gave a little whimper and slumped to the floor, dead. No doubt people would start taking their conscience a little more seriously.

In thinking about this, I recall a story I once read about the government's "Conscience Fund." The special account, which now totals more than several million dollars, was set up in 1813 for people like the woman who couldn't sleep at night because she'd reused an uncanceled stamp. This nagged at her periodically until she sent two stamps to the United States Treasury, along with a letter explaining what she had done. Then there's the individual who contributed $3,485 to make up for what he figured his laziness cost the government while he worked at a Veterans' Administration hospital.

I am ashamed to say it, but the "small wrongs" these people couldn't live with are not that different from the ones I often ignore or rationalize. Like Ananias and Sapphira, I sometimes fool myself into thinking that only the "big" transgressions matter and that true Christianity can be separated from following Christ's righteous pattern of life in very literal, everyday ways.

See also: Zechariah 8:16–17; Acts 24:16

WHAT THE WORLD NEEDS

Blessed is the man who does not walk in the counsel of the wicked or stand in the way of sinners or sit in the seat of mockers. But his delight is in the law of the Lord, and on his law he meditates day and night. He is like a tree planted by streams of water, which yields its fruit in season and whose leaf does not wither. Whatever he does prospers.

PSALM 1:1–3

The following words, written more than a century ago by Josiah Gilbert Holland, still seem appropriate today. No doubt they'll continue to be quoted one hundred years from now:

The world needs young men and women who cannot be bought; whose word is their bond; who put character above wealth; who possess opinions and a will; who are larger than their vocations; who do not hesitate to take chances.

The world needs young men and women who will not lose their individuality in a crowd; who will be as honest in small things as in great things; who will make no compromise with wrong; whose ambitions are not confined to their own selfish desires.

The world needs young men and women who will not say they do it because everybody else does it; who are true to their friends through good report and evil report, in adversity as well as in prosperity; who do not believe that shrewdness, cunning, and hard-headedness are the best qualities for winning; who are not ashamed or afraid to stand for the truth when it is unpopular.

The world needs young men and women who say no with emphasis, though all the rest of the world says yes.

See also: Psalm 34:19–22; 37

POINTS TO PONDER: CHARACTER

A good name is more desirable than great riches.

PROVERBS 22:1

Character is what you are in the dark.

DWIGHT L. MOODY

To murder character is as truly a crime as to murder the body: the tongue of the slanderer is brother to the dagger of the assassin.

TRYON EDWARDS

Merely going to church doesn't make you a Christian any more than going to a garage makes you an automobile.

BILLY SUNDAY

Reputation is what folks think you are. Personality is what you seem to be. Character is what you really are.

ALFRED ARMAND MONTAPERT

There is no such thing as a "self-made" man. We are made up of thousands of others. Everyone who has ever done a kind deed for us or spoken one word of encouragement to us, has entered into the make-up of our character and of our thoughts, as well as our success.

GEORGE MATTHEW ADAMS

If your absence doesn't make any difference, your presence won't either.

ANONYMOUS

Character is not made in a crisis—it is only exhibited.

ROBERT FREEMAN

It is one thing to go through a crisis grandly, but another thing to go through every day glorifying God when there is no witness, no limelight, no one paying the remotest attention to us.

OSWALD CHAMBERS

A good name, like good will, is got by many actions, and lost by one.

LORD JEFFREY

Nicknames stick to people, and the most ridiculous are the most adhesive.

THOMAS C. HALIBURTON

The reputation of a man is like his shadow: gigantic when it precedes him, and pygmy in its proportions when it follows.

ALEXANDRE DE TALLEYRAND-PERIGORD

The person who talks most of his own virtue is often the least virtuous.

JAWAHARLAL NEHRU

What people say behind your back is your standing in the community.

ED HOWE

Slanders are like flies that pass all over a man's good parts to light on his sores.

ANONYMOUS

When God measures a man, he puts the tape around the heart, not around the head.

ANONYMOUS

I have never felt that football built character. That is done by parents and church. You give us a boy with character and we will give you back a man. You give us a character—and we will give him right back to you.

JOHN MCKAY

A man is what he thinks about all day long.

RALPH WALDO EMERSON

The character of Jesus has not only been the highest pattern of virtue, but the strongest incentive to its practice, and has exerted so deep an influence that it may be truly said that the simple record of his three short years of active life has done more to regenerate and soften mankind than all the disquisitions of philosophers and the exhortations of moralists.

WILLIAM LECKY

See also: Acts 17:11; Romans 5:3–5; 1 Corinthians 15:33–34

WEEK

18

LOOKING AROUND

Do not merely listen to the word, and so deceive yourselves. Do what it says. Anyone who listens to the word but does not do what it says is like a man who looks at his face in a mirror and, after looking at himself, goes away and immediately forgets what he looks like. But the man who looks intently into the perfect law that gives freedom, and continues to do this, not forgetting what he has heard, but doing it–he will be blessed in what he does.

JAMES 1:22–25

Irene didn't have to look far to see some pretty pathetic examples of Christianity in action. For starters, there was the evening news broadcasts about the scandals involving prominent Christians. Closer to home, the wife of a church leader left her husband–not for another man, which would have been bad enough, but for another woman. On the school front, a group of teens who chirped about their Christianity maintained a clique that was pure bigotry toward outsiders. Not to mention Mr. Football, who acted like Jesus, Jr., during the week, but lived like the devil come Friday night.

Irene pointed out these phony Christians as a reason for not believing in Christ. I had to admit, she made a good case. But I also explained that these hypocrites did more to *prove* rather than disprove the existence of God.

To explain, I told her I'd started piano lessons a couple of weeks earlier. Though I'd never played before, my goal was to surprise my fiancée, who was a piano whiz, by memorizing just one song by Mozart. My efforts were pretty dismal, however, and the end result was not music. When I'd bang on the keyboard, dogs barked.

My awful example didn't mean everybody was equally bad at imitating Mozart. Nor did it mean others should think less of Mozart because of me, or doubt Mozart's existence. The fact that so many people, including lugs like myself, were trying to imitate his music indicates his true greatness.

A similar argument can be made about Jesus Christ. He has many imitators—some good, others bad. The fact that people don't imitate him perfectly is, of course, no reflection on him. Rather, as François de la Rochefoucauld has said, it is "the homage that vice pays to virtue."

In other words, bad people will always try acting like saints, which is a credit to Christ, not a detraction.

See also: Psalm 119:9–16; Matthew 7:17–23; Romans 2:21–24; 2 Corinthians 5:17–20

"FINE."

Encourage one another daily, as long as it is called Today, so that none of you may be hardened by sin's deceitfulness.

HEBREWS 3:13

It was easy to feel good about Sharon. All we ever did was go to movies, concerts, and football games. We scrambled from one date to another, too busy to spend much time talking or listening to each other about deeper things. When our dating relationship fizzled, I didn't feel I had ever really known her.

Shortly after we broke up she began dating somebody else. That romance soured before long, and I lost track of her for several months. When we eventually bumped into each other again, I asked how she was.

"Fine," she said, forcing a smile.

However, she wasn't fine. Another friend told me Sharon hadn't been around because she'd been fooling with razor blades, wondering how much she would bleed if she slashed her wrists. She experimented with a small cut and found that even a slight wound bled a lot. That scared her, so she swallowed a bottle of colored pills

229

instead. Thankfully, her parents found her in time and called an ambulance.

I couldn't figure out why Sharon would do something that stupid. She was a Christian and always seemed to have everything under control. But it was obvious I only knew the shell—the always-smiling, even-tempered, everything's-fine Sharon. On the inside she was a bloody mess.

The more I thought about her, the more I wondered about my other friends. None of us talked about our inner needs, doubts, or failings, so I naively assumed nobody had any. Was Sharon an exception, or were others struggling amidst their own private hell? If so, who? Who else needed my honest love and encouragement?

I didn't really know, so I had to suppose the answer was *everybody*. And then I asked God to help me be more caring in my friendships, indiscriminate in my love, and liberal in my compassion.

See also: Hebrews 10:24–25; 1 John 3:18

THE INNER CHAMBER

A man of many companions may come to ruin, but there is a friend who sticks closer than a brother.

PROVERBS 18:24

When it comes right down to it, most of us make pretty lousy friends. That probably has a lot to do with our desire for others to think we're better than we are.

Most of us want to be liked, but think nobody in their right mind would give us the time of day if they knew what we were really like. And so we keep most people at arm's length. That way they see just enough of us to think we're wonderful. And we don't risk them breaking through our high-gloss facade and bursting into that inner chamber where we sometimes think, feel, and act awfully desperate, unfriendly, and lonely.

Think about how conversations have gone with your friends during the past week. All too often they are shallow and cursory—the equivalent of caveman grunts:

"Dude!"

"Hey!"

"How's it going?"

"Not bad."

"Gotta blitz."

"Cool."

"Later."

As discussed yesterday, the end result of surface relationships is that we're appalled when someone like Sharon stumbles and behaves like an honest-to-goodness, imperfect human being. We somehow expect Christians to be always calm and emotionally controlled.

Unfortunately, we forget that each of us—you, me, your mom and dad, the new kid in town, your pastor—is in desperate, daily need of a Savior ... not to mention a good, old-fashioned friend to encourage us, talk about things that matter, help build our faith, and even explore the dark side of our souls.

Try making the first move. Ask God to help you select another mature individual with whom you can begin discussing your own areas of vulnerability. It will take time to develop this kind of close personal relationship. But it's a lot faster than waiting for somebody else to let down their guard first. In the latter case, the unfortunate reality is you'll likely be waiting the rest of your life.

See also: Proverbs 27:10; Romans 12:9–10

LOOKING FOR LOVE

He has rescued us from the dominion of darkness and brought us into the kingdom of the Son he loves, in whom we have redemption, the forgiveness of sins.

COLOSSIANS 1:13–14

It was summertime and the living was easy. As gorgeous weather raged outside, Bill Crawford was working on his second plate of ribs. Then he felt a tug on his sleeve and looked down at a four-year-old girl he'd never seen before. She was wearing a leopard-print bikini, and her arms were raised to be picked up.

He shook his head. "Not now, I'm eating," he said.

She tried the same thing with the other eighteen partygoers, but everybody was covered with barbecue sauce and wouldn't hold her.

A few minutes later somebody screamed. A man raced outside and dove into the pool. When he surfaced, he held the limp body of the little girl in his arms. Somebody started mouth-to-mouth, but she was dead before the ambulance arrived.

"She did the same thing last week," somebody whispered as they carried away her body.

"And twice the week before that," another said quietly.

Before long, Bill had pieced together the story. She was illegitimate and unloved, and a couple of months earlier she'd accidentally fallen into the pool. Upon being rescued, she'd won instant love and attention which she never experienced at home. So she tried the trick three more times in subsequent weeks, and it always worked.

On the day of the barbecue, when nobody picked her up, she resorted to the only sure way she knew to capture attention. Unfortunately, this time it didn't work.

Bill couldn't think of the girl without concluding she wasn't alone. Many other people he knew were desperate for love and acceptance. Perhaps they didn't throw themselves into backyard pools, but they did plunge into drugs, alcohol, sex—anything that would give them the feeling of belonging. But the very thing they saw as the solution eventually destroyed them.

"It wasn't the swimming pool that provided that little girl with love and acceptance," Bill said, looking back on the tragedy. "It was the person who jumped in and saved her from it."

I believe that's the great thing about Christianity. Jesus Christ jumped into the world to save us from drowning. He wants to offer us the love and care and feelings we're searching for.

"Unlike those of us at the party," he added, "Jesus won't ignore or turn away anyone."

See also: Luke 19:10; Romans 7:24–25; 1 Timothy 1:15

SOUNDS OF SILENCE

Be still before the Lord, all mankind.

ZECHARIAH 2:13

In the middle of the Indiana woods sits a tiny hut constructed of rubble scrounged from nearby building sites. Resembling a toolshed more than anything habitable, it represents the major turning point in the life of John Michael Talbot, a born-again, guitar-playing Franciscan monk who called the shack "home" for one bone-numbing winter after everything in his life fell apart. Alone, in solitude, he sought God.

At first he had romantic thoughts about living as a hermit and being "spiritual," but he was cured of that the first day his beard froze.

"I spent a good part of the morning just trying to get a flame kindled," he told me. "And most of the rest of the day revolved around chopping wood, nursing fires, praying, and watching squirrels."

But after you've seen a squirrel do everything a squirrel does, what else is there? Before long he began to experience good, basic boredom. And he discovered the true meaning of loneliness.

"I'd read the Scriptures and think, 'I've read this before. I don't need to read it again.' But it was during these basic, boring days that I experienced a deeper sense of just *being*. And in my silence I heard God's most profound words."

John Michael admitted that people aren't going to rush out and build Daniel Boone huts in the woods just to experience some spiritual dimension of silence. But he also said they don't have to. They can easily experience it where they are.

"There's always things that compete with that stillness," he said. "It can be a stereo or TV. The key is not necessarily to build a hermitage. It may start with discovering how to use a stereo and TV properly, or learning how to turn them off. It may be taking a walk around the neighborhood, looking and listening, contemplating what you see in light of God. It might be to spend some time near a creek or park, learning how God communicates through silence. 'It's taking time to be still.'"

See also: Psalm 23:1–3; 37:7; Zephaniah 3:17

SOLITARY CONFINEMENT

My soul is downcast within me. Yet this I call to mind and therefore I have hope: Because of the Lord's great love we are not consumed, for his compassions never fail. They are new every morning; great is your faithfulness. I say to myself, "The Lord is my portion; therefore I will wait for him." The Lord is good to those whose hope is in him, to the one who seeks him; it is good to wait quietly for the salvation of the Lord.

LAMENTATIONS 3:20–26

Being alone can be the worst feeling in the world. It's watching everybody else pair off at the party while you keep the corner company. It's trying to figure out how you'd respond if your parents ever said they loved you. It's breaking up and suddenly spending weekends in the solitary confinement of your room.

Being alone is running for the phone every time it rings, hoping that just once somebody will ask for you. It's hearing yourself referred to over the loudspeakers: "Fumble, number thirty-two." It's looking down into the casket of a friend or relative. It's being stranded on the freeway at eleven o'clock at night. It's being pregnant and unmarried.

Being alone is looking in the mirror, trying to imagine yourself looking like anybody but yourself. It's watching the taillights of your best friend's car as her family moves two thousand miles away. It's telling a door-to-door salesman about your life because nobody else seems to care.

Being alone forces you to confront yourself. It loosens your grip on all surroundings and props, and temporarily frees you from things you generally rely on or deem important.

Being alone drives you to examine what really matters. It forces your values and fears and insecurities out of the shadows and into the light, enabling you to see things about yourself and others that you might not otherwise get to know. For example, why do your parents find it so hard to express love? Maybe they never really learned how. Maybe they need you to take the first step.

As such, being alone is an *opportunity*—an opportunity to listen to yourself and to God, to let the fog in your life lift and the mud settle, to get your bearings and again draw near to God.

The opportunities are pretty common; they're before you every day. It's the people who recognize and know how to seize them that are rare.

See also: Psalm 68:5–6; Luke 5:16

POINTS TO PONDER: LONELINESS

Where can I go from your Spirit? Where can I flee from your presence? If I go up to the heavens, you are there; if I make my bed in the depths, you are there. If I rise on the wings of the dawn, if I settle on the far side of the sea, even there your hand will guide me, your right hand will hold me fast.

PSALM 139:7–10

The soul hardly ever realizes it, but whether he is a believer or not, his loneliness is really a homesickness for God.

HUBERT VAN ZELLER

People are lonely because they build walls instead of bridges.

JOSEPH F. NEWTON

If you were not strangers here, the hounds of the world would not bark at you.

SAMUEL RUTHERFORD

Hell is eternal separation from the presence of the Lord.

V. RAYMOND EDMAN

The whole conviction of my life now rests upon the belief that loneliness, far from being a rare and curious phenomenon, peculiar to myself and to a few other solitary men, is the central and inevitable fact of human existence.

THOMAS WOLFE

The deepest need of man is the need to overcome his separateness, to leave the prison of his aloneness.

ERICH FROMM

It is easy in the world to live after the world's opinions; it is easy in solitude to live after your own; but the great man is he who in the midst of the crowd keeps with perfect sweetness the independence of solitude.

RALPH WALDO EMERSON

Loneliness is the first thing which God's eye nam'd not good.

JOHN MILTON

The mission of Jesus cannot be defined without speaking of man being lost.

HENRI BLOCHER

Students today live in a generation of alienation. Alienation in the ghettos, alienation in the university, alienation from parents, alienation on every side. Sometimes [they] forget that the basic alienation with which they are faced is a cosmic alienation ... [They feel] there is nobody home in the universe.

FRANCES A. SCHAEFFER

In cities no one is quiet but many are lonely; in the country, people are quiet but few are lonely.

GEOFFREY FRANCIS FISHER

Solitude is essential to man. All men come into this world alone and leave it alone.

THOMAS DE QUINCEY

My heart is a lonely hunter that hunts on a lonely hill.

WILLIAM SHARP

The surest cure for vanity is loneliness.

THOMAS WOLFE

Man's sin problem is never cured until his alienation from God is overcome, until the rebellion of the human against the divine is ended, until God and man are brought back together.

MYRON S. AUGSBURGER

I was never less alone than when by myself.

EDWARD GIBBON

Shakespeare, Leonardo da Vinci, Benjamin Franklin, and Lincoln ... were not afraid of being lonely because they knew that was when the creative mood in them would work.

CARL SANDBURG

The more affluent a society is, the more pronounced is the sense of ultimate emptiness and alienation on the part of its members.

BILLY GRAHAM

Language has created the word loneliness to express the pain of being alone, and the word solitude to express the glory of being alone.

PAUL TILLICH

See also: Joshua 1:5–9; Psalm 25:16–18

WEEK

19

SOLEMN VOWS

> *As a bridegroom rejoices over his bride, so will your God rejoice over you.*
>
> Isaiah 62:5

Behind me rose the church altar. Before me sat a crowd of three hundred friends and relatives. Beside me stood the young woman, gowned in white and bearing a wisp of a smile, who would soon be my wife. But first there was the matter of vows. Slowly, and with a somewhat trembling voice, I turned to Julie and said:

"I take thee, Julie, to be my lawfully wedded wife, to have and to hold from this day forward; for better, for worse; for richer, for poorer; in sickness and in heath; to love and to cherish, till death us do part."

My voice wasn't shaking because of the crowd, but because I was unsure of what the future held. At twenty-one I was making a vow of love that would bridge the bad times, the lean times, the ill times until we were parted by death—and only by death.

There was no guarantee our lives would be rosy and bright. That was the risk. Nevertheless, I vowed to love her, *no matter what.* I did it with a fair share of nervousness, yes; but a bigger share, by far, of unadorned, stand-up-and-holler enthusiasm.

As soon as the words were out of my mouth, however, the most amazing thing happened. Julie vowed the exact same thing! She pledged her very life—to *me!*

As I look back on that very special day, I can't help but think how similar my marriage vows were to my commitment to Christ. When I made that decision at seventeen, I was nervous then, too. I didn't know what lay ahead. And there were risks. But I vowed to love God with all my heart, with all my mind, and with all my soul—*no matter what.* Likewise, God pledged to accept me unconditionally, for better, for worse, for richer, for poorer, in sickness and in health.

The difference, of course, is that my bond with God lasts forever. It's not a case of "until death us do part." That's just when things start looking up—the point I finally meet the bridegroom face-to-face.

See also: Matthew 25:1–10; Revelation 21

INSIDE OUT

God does not judge by external appearance.

GALATIANS 2:6

Gregg and Shelly were probably the happiest couple I ever knew. They became friends through church in their junior years, and their relationship grew to be "more than friends" over the summer when they shared a biology class.

Shelly was Miss Personality and had cover-girl looks to match. She was the kind of person you could talk to for five minutes and feel like you'd known her all your life. She oozed enthusiasm and talked with exclamation points. As for Gregg, he was no slouch in the personality department, though he tended to have a quieter disposition than Shelly and a subtler sense of humor. But when it came to looks, he was far from being the major, all-American stud that Shelly normally hung around with. On the surface at least, they were a clear mismatch.

However, Shelly was enormously happy in Gregg's company and didn't give a second thought to his bird legs or his honk of a nose or anything else. Nor did she think twice about the guys she stopped dead in their tracks whenever she passed. For her, looks were superficial. Though her friends sometimes commented about Gregg's appearance, she let it be known that she loved and respected him for who he was on the inside. That is, for his integrity, his compassion, the way he encouraged her when she was down, and his deep Christian roots. "As for the legs," she'd say, "I think they're kind of cute."

In the Bible, surface appearance doesn't count for much. Samuel was reminded of that when he went to anoint a new king over Israel. Samuel wanted a Sylvester Stallone; God wanted David.

"Do not consider his appearance or his height," the Lord said to Samuel. "The Lord does not look at the things man looks at. Man looks at the outward appearance, but the Lord looks at the heart."

It's a classic message—one well worth remembering.

See also: 1 Samuel 16:7; Psalm 147:10−11; Luke 16:15

BLAME IT ON BOOZE

Wine is a mocker and beer a brawler; whoever is led astray by them is not wise.

PROVERBS 20:1

Like a jug of Gallo wine, King Xerxes was all neck and belly. He had no head. Historians of his day portrayed him as impulsive, wild, dangerous. When a bridge he had erected was wiped out by high water, it's recorded that he ordered the sea to be whipped three hundred times, and then had the bridge builders beheaded. When he sobered up, he probably blamed his ridiculous actions on booze.

Being married to an alcoholic can be sheer hell on earth. And the life of Xerxes' wife, Vashti, was no exception. When he headed for the wine cellar, she headed for the door. He interpreted such behavior as feminist independence; Vashti saw it as survival. She probably just didn't want to get beaten up.

Perhaps to generate points with the menfolk in town, or maybe just because he didn't like to drink alone, King Xerxes threw open both the palace and wine cellar doors to every male in town. For an entire week, drinks were on the house: "wine was served in goblets of gold, each one different from the other, and the royal wine was abundant, in keeping with the king's liberality" (Esther 1:7). In addition, "each guest was allowed to drink in his own way, for the king instructed all the wine stewards to serve each man what he wished" (Esther 1:8).

About the time Xerxes started seeing pink elephants, he summoned his wife to parade in front of his pie-eyed male friends. Vashti had a figure that would stop a chariot, but she also had a brain to match and wasn't about to strut in front of a bunch of drunk, male chauvinist pigs. So she did the only thing she could think of: she sent a message to the king, politely telling him to take a flying leap.

With his ego now as smashed as he was, Xerxes decided to make an example of Vashti in case other women got any funny ideas and refused to let their alcoholic husbands humiliate them in public. He divorced her on the spot.

For Vashti, it wasn't much of a loss; Xerxes had always preferred the company of a bottle over her, anyway. And though suddenly stripped of her crown, she wore her integrity like a golden tiara.

See also: Esther 1; Romans 13:11–14; Ephesians 5:18

EMPTY EYES

For this reason a man will leave his father and mother and be united to his wife, and they will become one flesh.

GENESIS 2:24

The way Elisa told it, it was really "no big deal." When she first learned she was pregnant by Chuck, she began psyching herself up to have the baby adopted. So she was mostly ready when the big moment arrived and the nurses took away the newborn without letting her see whether it was a boy or a girl.

Elisa had quit school to live with Chuck and wait for the delivery. He teased her about "playing house" when she refinished the dresser and patched a gash in the window shade. But any suggestion that they get married was treated more like a joke than anything else. The nine months dragged along, as did their relationship, and most of their time together was spent arguing and fighting and watching television on hot sticky nights in his hole-in-the-wall apartment.

When Elisa came home from the hospital, Chuck was living with another girl—somebody from work. So Elisa took a job working tables at a little cafe and rented a room with a half bath and hot plate. "It was no big deal," she said.

Before long she began sleeping with Glen, an Army private who was passing through on a short leave. Their relationship was pretty uncomplicated, in part because it didn't have time to get complicated. She was just happy to have somebody hold her through the long nights and promise to write her from overseas.

Elisa more or less took things as they came, and did her best to laugh it off when she talked about the problems and emptiness and hurts in her life. But they were choking, panicky laughs, which caused her eyes to flood. She dabbed away the tears with a strand of hair while trying hard to convince herself that everything would be fine if she just laughed a little more and kept her eyes dry and tried not to think about life or love all that much, or about the Cinderella dreams and white picket fence hopes she'd had for herself as a little girl.

Aside from the tears, her eyes were as empty as any of the old boxes that cluttered her closets, waiting for the next move. She said it was all really no big deal, but her eyes gave her away. They spoke sermons about what happens when sex is separated from love and commitment.

And if you'd ever want to know why God created the protective haven of marriage, a look deep into Elisa's eyes would give you a pretty good idea.

See also: Proverbs 5:18–23; 1 Corinthians 6:18–20; Philippians 1:27

LOVE FOR A LIFETIME

If I speak in the tongues of men and of angels, but have not love, I am only a resounding gong or a clanging cymbal. If I have the gift of prophecy and can fathom all mysteries and all knowledge, and if I have a faith that can move mountains, but have not love, I am nothing. If I give all I possess to the poor and surrender my body to the flames, but have not love, I gain nothing.

1 CORINTHIANS 13:1–3

Romantic love is probably the biggest lift in life. It gives you a buzz clear to the bones and brightens the landscape around you. Even in the dead of winter, you feel like the middle of spring. Trees seem greener, the flowers brighter, and tomorrow's history exam less threatening.

But true love, if it is indeed true, is more than emotional rush. Good-time feelings come and go, but love endures only if it's nurtured in an environment of *trust, respect,* and *sacrifice.*

Without trust, love erodes. Trust says: I will remove all "No Trespassing" signs from our relationship, not demand we spend every minute together, and give you the freedom God does—to return my love if you so choose. I will allow you to be yourself—at the risk of knowing others may be attracted to the very things that attracted me.

Without respect, love withers. Respect says: I will honor your privacy, listen to your thoughts, learn from our differences, and treat your body like God does—as the temple of the Holy Spirit. I won't try to mold you in my image; doing so would merely ensure one of us isn't needed.

Without sacrifice, love dies. Sacrifice says: I will relinquish the masks that shield my deepest, most confusing emotions; sur-

245

render my pride that refuses to be hurt; and share completely the roller-coaster adventure of seeking God's highest calling for each of our lives. I will forget about love being a fifty-fifty proposition, and contribute my *best* to the relationship—even if you're unable to love me back.

Yes, I will love you completely—in an environment of trust, respect, and sacrifice—no strings attached. After all, that's how God first loved us.

See also: John 13:34–35; 1 Corinthians 13:4–7; 1 John 3:11–23

THE PERFECT GIFT

Marriage should be honored by all, and the marriage bed kept pure, for God will judge the adulterer and all the sexually immoral.

HEBREWS 13:4

Talking on the phone with Patti was so natural that John felt they were made for each other. And after a half-dozen dates which ended with neither of them wanting to say good-night, he knew he was in love.

To express the depth of his love for Patti, John decided to make something special. And so he bought an expensive block of imported wood from which he began carving a pair of lovebirds. For weeks he worked long into the night, cutting, shaping, and sanding. When finished, the lovebirds were so beautiful he cried. Patti cried, too, when she opened the box. It was the perfect gift.

Spring approached, and with it came the promise of warmer weather. But ice was forming on John and Patti's relationship, and they didn't survive the chill. On the rebound John fell head over heels in love with Laura. He waited a few months, and then considered ways to display his feelings. He searched the malls, but no store-bought present would do. In the end, he could settle for nothing less than making another pair of lovebirds.

A few years and several sets of lovebirds later, John met the woman he wanted to marry. Lisa was everything he'd hoped for in a mate, and all of his other relationships seemed like puppy loves by comparison. Some of their happiest times were spent picking out wedding rings together, and even though John splurged in a big way, he longed to do something more for Lisa.

And so it was that he labored long into the cold nights with his chisels and blades. When he finally presented the lovebirds to Lisa on their wedding night, she smiled broadly and told him there wasn't a happier woman in all the world.

He watched her eyes closely, wondering if she knew of the other lovebirds. And when she held her pair up into the light, he couldn't help thinking of Patti and Laura and all of the other girls he'd given the same present to.

He'd wanted to give his bride something more special and unique. But how could he have improved on the perfect gift?

See also: 1 Corinthians 6:18–20; Ephesians 5:3; 1 Thessalonians 4:3–8

POINTS TO PONDER:
LOVE AND SEX

At the beginning of creation God "made them male and female." "For this reason a man will leave his father and mother and be united to his wife, and the two will become one flesh." So they are no longer two, but one. Therefore what God has joined together, let man not separate.

MARK 10:6–9

There is no surprise more magical than the surprise of being loved. It is the finger of God on a man's shoulder.

CHARLES MORGAN

Sex is a flame which uncontrolled may scorch; properly guided, it will light the torch of eternity.

JOSEPH FETTERMAN

A successful marriage is an edifice that must be rebuilt every day.

ANDRE MAUROIS

There are three kinds of love: false, natural, and married. False love is that which seeks its own, just as one loves gold, goods, honour, or women outside of matrimony contrary to God's command. Natural love is between father and children, brother and sister. But above them all is married love. It burns as fire, and seeks nothing more than the mate. It says, "I wish not yours; I wish neither gold nor silver, neither this nor that. I want only you."

MARTIN LUTHER

Of all powers, love is the most powerful and the most powerless. It is the most powerful because it alone can conquer that final and most impregnable stronghold which is the human heart. It is the most powerless because it can do nothing except by consent.

FREDERICK BUECHNER

In marriage, being the right person is as important as finding the right person.

WILBERT DONALD GOUGH

Modern man refuses to recognize that God has set certain standards, certain absolutes for sex, as he has for behavior generally. To be ignorant of these absolutes, or to deny them or rationalize them, in no way invalidates them.

L. NELSON BELL

The difficulty with marriage is that we fall in love with a personality, but must live with a character.

PETER DEVRIES

If there is anything better than to be loved, it is to love.

ANONYMOUS

A happy marriage is the union of two good forgivers.

ROBERT QUILLEN

Contrary to Mrs. Gundy, sex is not sin. Contrary to Hugh Hefner, it's not salvation either. Like nitro-glycerine, it can be used either to blow up bridges or heal hearts.

FREDERICK BUECHNER

Love built on beauty, soon as beauty, dies.

JOHN DONNE

One of the great similarities between Christianity and marriage is that, for Christians, they both get better as we get older.

JEAN A. REES

We may, indeed, be sure that perfect chastity—like perfect charity—will not be attained by any merely human efforts. You must ask for God's help. Even when you have done so, it may seem to you for a long time that no help, or less help than you need, is being given. Never mind. After each failure, ask forgiveness, pick yourself up, and try again. Very often what God first helps us towards is not the virtue itself but just this power of always trying again. For however important chastity (or courage, or truthfulness, or any other virtue) may be, this process trains us in habits of the soul which are more important still. It cures our illusions about ourselves and teaches us to depend on God. We learn, on the one hand, that we cannot trust ourselves even in our best moments, and, on the other, that we need not despair even in our worst, for our failures are forgiven. The only fatal thing is to sit down content with anything less than perfection.

C. S. LEWIS

There is a tendency to think of sex as something degrading; it is not, it is magnificent, an enormous privilege, but because of that the rules are tremendously strict and severe.

FRANCES DEVAS

I never knew how to worship until I knew how to love.

HENRY WARD BEECHER

The heart of marriage is its communication system. It can be said that the success and happiness of any married pair is measurable in terms of the deepening dialogue which characterizes their union.

DWIGHT SMALL

We pray that the young men and women of today and tomorrow will grow up with the realization that sex is a beautiful flame they carry in the lantern of their bodies.

DEMETRIUS MONOUSOS

Love is not blind—it sees more, not less. But because it sees more, it is willing to see less.

RABBI JULIUS GORDON

God help the man who won't marry until he finds a perfect woman, and God help him still more if he finds her.

BENJAMIN TILLETT

See also: Matthew 5:27–30; 1 Corinthians 13; Ephesians 5:1–17

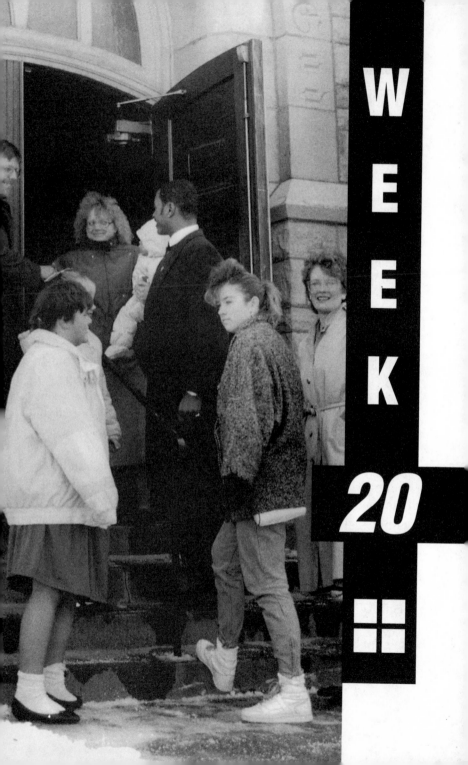

WEEK

20

FITTING THE MOLD

For it is by grace you have been saved, through faith – and this not from yourselves, it is the gift of God – not by works, so that no one can boast. For we are God's workmanship, created in Christ Jesus to do good works, which God prepared in advance for us to do.

EPHESIANS 2:8–10

Keith thought he knew exactly how a Christian should look and behave. For starters, he looked harried because he was always running late to a blur of Bible studies, discipleship classes, choir practices, and prayer meetings. He described himself as a "one-hundred-percent-sold-out-for-Jesus, born-again believer."

As such, Keith behaved like a stage-ten idiot. He referred to various teachers as "pagans" and to students he passed in the hall, he'd blurt, "You must be born again!" And he said it with a straight face. One day he outdid himself and tried to command an "evil spirit" to come out of another student during lunch, but only succeeded in being slugged in the jaw. After he picked himself off the ground, he walked away muttering, "Bless those who curse you, pray for those who mistreat you."

His behavior reminds me of a story told by Richard Foster about a wealthy man who ordered a handmade suit from Hans, a renowned tailor. When the man stopped by to pick up the suit, he noticed that one shoulder caved in, while the other bulged out. The sleeves were sewn to the back and front rather than the sides of the coat. And the pant legs were cockeyed and short. But the man didn't want to make a fuss, so he said nothing. He stepped into the dressing room and, after a long period of painful twisting and shoving, managed to fit the convoluted pattern.

After admiring himself in the mirror, he paid the tailor and caught a bus home. Fellow passengers kept staring at the man, until one finally tapped him on the shoulder and asked if Hans hadn't made his new suit. Receiving a nod, he replied, "Amazing! I knew

Hans was a great tailor, but I had no idea he could make a suit to fit someone as deformed as you!"

Like Keith, we all appear somewhat deformed whenever we think of Christianity as a set of external actions, as a way to look or act. Too often we bruise and batter ourselves to fit illogical molds of behavior. But thankfully we are human *beings*, not *doings*. Even more thankfully, Christianity is not based on anything we do. We can't push and shove our way closer to God.

As Paul wrote in the verses above, true spirituality isn't a matter of works and wilpower on our part, but grace on God's part. He simply draws close to our side. Almost unaware, we're overcome by a growing sense of awe and reverence, and we begin to experience a lifechange—from the inside out.

See also: Romans 3:10–12; Ephesians 2:1–10; Philippians 2:13

ONLY THE FACTS

There is no one righteous, not even one; there is no one who understands, no one who seeks God. All have turned away, they have together become worthless; there is no one who does good, not even one.

ROMANS 3:10–12

Just about everything these days has been quantified, surveyed, indexed, tabulated, and spewed out in one official document or another. This torrent of data informs us, often to our dismay, what we are truly like. For example, I recently read in the paper that:

- Exactly 68 percent of American children live with both of their biological parents; the percentage of Americans who don't recognize CBS News Anchorman Dan Rather is 55; and 42 percent of Americans regularly attend religious services.

- The probability of dying from unnatural causes on your next commercial jet flight is about one in seven million. Even if you fly daily, you can expect to meet the grim reaper aboard only once in every 19,000 years.
- Of white-collar workers in America, 49 percent say they are cyberphobic or resistant to new technology; 66 percent don't use electronic mail or carry beepers; 65 percent use personal computers; and 58 percent haven't heard anything about the Internet.
- There are 105 different familial relationships for which Hallmark makes cards; when conversing with the opposite sex, males make 96 percent of all interruptions; and the number of schools that invited Lee Iacocca to speak at their graduation in June 1986 was 150.

It is common knowledge that ours is the best informed generation in history—even though 82.6 percent of us probably can't locate Iran on a map, explain exactly what a catalytic converter does, or name the second president of the United States.

What is important is not so much the volume of information that bombards us (we're hit by far more than anyone could absorb, anyway) but *which* statistics we act on. For example, it's unimportant whether you know the name Lee Iacocca and how many speaking invitations he received way back when. There are no consequences if you ignore such information. But some statistics are a matter of life and death. For example:

- The number of people who have sinned and fall short of the glory of God is 100 percent;
- The number of people who are destined to die once, and after that to face judgment is 100 percent;
- At the name of Jesus, the number of knees that will bow, in heaven and on earth and under the earth, and the number of tongues that will confess Jesus Christ as Lord is also 100 percent.

With God, there are no loopholes. It's all or nothing—100 percent of the time.

See also: Romans 3:23; Hebrews 9:27; Philippians 2:10–11

NO EXCUSE

> *You, therefore, have no excuse, you who pass judgment on someone else, for at whatever point you judge the other, you are condemning yourself, because you who pass judgment do the same things.*

ROMANS 2:1

It has been quite some time since I thought much about the hypocrisy around me. Sure, I know it's there. I read the newspapers, listen to the news, hear snatches of gossip. But there's enough hypocrisy in my own life to consume most all of my attention and, presumably, quite a bit of God's as well.

While we tend to judge each other based on outward appearances (whether we act secure, witty, spiritual, etc.), the Lord judges the heart. And we can't mask our innermost thoughts and feelings to fool him. He knows even the best of us harbor secret thoughts of hatred, pride, and lust—inner sins that only he can deal with. Who are we to pretend they don't exist?

Because of this perspective, Christ levels the boom on those who worry about others' problems: "Don't pick on people, jump on their failures, criticize their faults—unless, of course, you want the same treatment," he challenged. "That critical spirit has a way of boomeranging. It's easy to see a smudge on your neighbor's face and be oblivious to the ugly sneer on your own. Do you have the nerve to say, 'Let me wash your face for you,' when your own face is distorted by contempt? It's this whole traveling road-show mentality all over again, playing a holier-than-thou part instead of just living your part. Wipe that ugly sneer off your own face, and you might be fit to offer a washcloth to your neighbor" (Matthew 7:1–5 *The Message*).

It's not that God wants us to be blind to sin and hypocrisy around us. The Bible repeatedly urges believers to evaluate people and situations carefully, to choose between good and evil. We are warned about sexually immoral people (1 Corinthians 5:9) and "angels of light" (2 Corinthians 11:14), among others, and urged to "test everything" (1 Thessalonians 5:21).

Nevertheless, we should quit focusing our binoculars on others' sin and hypocrisy when we have trouble seeing the same things in the mirror.

See also: Luke 6:37–38; Romans 14:10–13; 1 Corinthians 4:5

INTELLECTUAL HONESTY

Where is the wise man? Where is the scholar? Where is the philosopher of this age? Has not God made foolish the wisdom of the world? For since in the wisdom of God the world through its wisdom did not know him, God was pleased through the foolishness of what was preached to save those who believe.

1 CORINTHIANS 1:20–21

As Maxine Hancock tells the story, she was on her way to Anthropology 378 when her friend, Dave, invited her to a noon Bible study on campus. About half a dozen others would be there, he said.

"Bible study?" she hooted. "Why study *that?*"

Dave smiled, mumbled something about how if she'd come once or twice she'd understand why, and just kept walking. Not wanting to end the conversation so abruptly, Maxine tried another angle.

"You know, Dave, I don't really think that an intellectually honest person can take the Bible seriously anymore." He didn't respond, so she continued. "Let's face it, everybody knows about the contradictions." She did a quick mental search for an example in case Dave asked, but couldn't think of anything offhand. No matter; he let it pass. "And the myths like Adam and Eve and Noah and the boys. I just don't see that it's honest to go on taking an outmoded book so seriously. That's all."

By the time they were almost to class, Dave had still not responded. She figured she'd gotten his goat, and that it would be a long while before he asked her to something similar again. Maybe he'd even skip the noon study himself and take her out to lunch instead—something she was more interested in.

When Dave finally spoke up, he cleared his throat as if he was going to talk about something else. "Say, Maxine," he said, "speaking of intellectual honesty. . ."

She fell for it hard. "Yeah?" she said, glancing up.

"What do you think about somebody doing a critical review of a book she's never read?"

See also: Isaiah 29:14–16; 1 Corinthians 1:26–31; 2:6–16

CARRYING ON THE JOB

The body is a unit, though it is made up of many parts; and though all its parts are many, they form one body. So it is with Christ. For we were all baptized by one Spirit into one body—whether Jews or Greeks, slave or free—and we were all given the one Spirit to drink.

1 CORINTHIANS 12:12–13

I once had a boss who agreed to contribute an article for a book but couldn't find time to write the piece. The day before it was due, something came up and he had to catch a plane out of town. I asked him about the article. "Why don't you write it for me," he said. And then he was gone.

The assignment was an act of trust more than anything else. He could have written the article on the plane or in his hotel room that night, but he wanted to involve me. And he knew he could trust me to speak for him.

Christ entrusted us with a similar assignment shortly before he returned to heaven. For thirty-three years he walked the earth, providing people with a close-up look at God. If you wanted to know what God was like, all you had to do was take a good look at Jesus. For the first time, God was more than a voice in the clouds or a dusty concept in a scroll. He had a body, a face.

When Jesus ascended into heaven, he did not vacate Planet Earth. Rather, he left his followers behind, filled them with his Spirit, and asked them to serve for him, love for him, speak for him.

We carry on that job—in his name. Now, as then, we are his body, his hands, his eyes, his heart. Our actions, words, morals, and thoughts should all mirror his character. If we are successful, people around us will recognize God and want to know him. If they fail to recognize him, could it be we're not doing our job?

See also: Matthew 28:18–20; Acts 1:8; Colossians 3:17

■■

THE PERFECT JOB

Your attitude should be the same as that of Christ Jesus: Who, being in very nature God, did not consider equality with God something to be grasped, but made himself nothing, taking the very nature of a servant, being made in human likeness. And being found in appearance as a man, he humbled himself and became obedient to death—even death on a cross!

PHILIPPIANS 2:5–8

The job description seemed easy enough: live in Hawaii and play Santa Claus to the poor. But it turned out harder than Linda imagined.

The work took her into the poorest sections, where the flies outnumbered people one hundred to one, where a stench hung in the air because the streets were treated like one big dumpster, where the worry of parents who didn't have enough to feed their children was almost palpable, and where the hungry children had stopped crying because crying only made them hungrier.

With barking dogs on her heels and a burning sun on her back, Linda trudged into the barrios to tell immigrants about the no-cost services provided by the government: free driving lessons, medical insurance, Kung Fu classes, even free college education—not to mention dental care at less than a dollar per visit. She thought it was an offer nobody could refuse. But in the end, most of the people she was supposed to help didn't want help. They were suspicious and afraid, and time after time they shut their rickety doors in her face.

Why not spare the hassle and drudgery and just print up a flyer? she thought. A little brochure describing all of the services could easily be left on people's doorsteps. That way it wouldn't be any sweat off her back if people didn't want help. As it was, the person-to-person visits were *killing* her.

But then another thought struck her. What if Jesus had skipped the visit and sent flyers instead? What if all you had to do to become a Christian was return a postage-paid coupon? It would have been so much easier than hassling with the crowds. It would have been so much easier than bothering with the cross.

See also: John 15:13; Romans 5:6–8; 1 John 4:9–10

POINTS TO PONDER: JUDGMENT

Since you call on a Father who judges each man's work impartially, live your lives as strangers here in reverent fear. For you know that it was not with perishable things such as silver or gold that you were redeemed from the empty way of life handed down to you from your forefathers, but with the precious blood of Christ, a lamb without blemish or defect.

1 PETER 1:17–19

He who has spoken in love will soon be obliged to speak in judgment.

KAY GUDNASON

The New Testament proclaims that at some unforeseeable time in the future God will bring down the final curtain on history, and there will come a Day on which all our days and all the judgments upon us and all our judgments upon each other will themselves be judged. The judge will be Christ. In other words, the one who judges us most finally will be the one who loves us most fully.

FREDERICK BUECHNER

There is no fear of judgment for the man who judges himself according to the Word of God.

HOWARD G. HENDRICKS

You shall judge a man by his foes as well as by his friends.

JOSEPH CONRAD

Truly at the day of judgment we shall not be examined on what we have read, but what we have done; not how well we have spoken, but how religiously we have lived.

THOMAS À KEMPIS

The average man's judgment is so poor, he runs a risk every time he uses it.

ED HOWE

We are all of us judged every day. We are judged by the face that looks back at us from the bathroom mirror. We are judged by the faces of the people we love and by the faces and lives of our children and by our dreams. Each day finds us at the junction of many roads, and we are judged as much by the roads we have not taken as by the roads we have.

FREDERICK BUECHNER

Don't wait for the Last Judgment. It takes place every day.

ALBERT CAMUS

Hesitancy in judgment is the only true mark of the thinker.

DAGOBERT D. RUNES

We should quit focusing our binoculars on others' sin and hypocrisy when we have trouble seeing the same things in the mirror.

S. RICKLY CHRISTIAN

The promises of sin are fair, but the payoff is cruel.

ALBERT NIELSEN

We judge ourselves by what we feel capable of doing; others judge us by what we have done.

HENRY WADSWORTH LONGFELLOW

History shows that Christ on the cross has been more potent than anything else in arousing a compassion for suffering and indignation at injustice.

F. J. FOAKES-JACKSON

Romantic love is blind to everything except what is lovable and lovely, but Christ's love sees us with terrible clarity and sees us whole. Christ's love so wishes our joy that it is ruthless against everything in us that diminishes our joy. The worst sentence Love can pass is that we behold the suffering which Love has endured for our sake, and that is also our acquittal. The justice and mercy of the judge are ultimately one.

FREDERICK BUECHNER

A man's judgment of another depends more on the one judging and on his passions than on the one being judged and his conduct.

PAUL TOURNIER

I believe the troubles that have come upon us are in part a judgment of God on us for our sins; and that unless we repent and turn to God we are finished as a free democratic society.

BILLY GRAHAM

Indeed, I tremble for my country when I reflect that God is just.

THOMAS JEFFERSON

Only the sinner has a right to preach.

CHRISTOPHER MORLEY

See also: John 3:16–17; 8:3–7; Romans 2:1–6; Hebrews 9:27–28

WEEK

21

THIRD GRADE MATH

> *Caiaphas, who was high priest that year, spoke up,*
> *"You know nothing at all! You do not realize that it is bet-*
> *ter for you that one man die for the people than that the*
> *whole nation perish."*

> JOHN 11:49–50

Caiaphas was essentially the Jewish equivalent of the pope. As the religious boss man of Israel, he presided over the high court of the Jews, called the Sanhedrin. For the most part, he kept things quiet on the home front, and the Roman feds pretty much stayed out of his hair and left him to his cushy job.

However, Caiaphas began to sweat as Jesus headed toward Jerusalem after three years of stirring up controversy and converts around the countryside. By the time he'd fed the five thousand and raised Lazarus from the dead, he was a household name. So the throngs were waiting when he hit Main Street, and they gave him the equivalent of a ticker-tape parade.

Caiaphas and members of the Sanhedrin were also waiting —not to celebrate, but to capture; not to congratulate, but to crucify. They had their reasons to be hot and bothered by the blue-collar Jew. These probably had less to do with his claiming equality with God and healing people on the Sabbath than his habit of talking about religious honchos in less than complimentary terms. He'd singled out these sanctimonious sourpusses as being proud and petty, and they had their fill of it.

"If we let him go on, pretty soon everyone will be believing in him and the Romans will come and remove what little power and privilege we still have," they fretted (John 11:48 *The Message*).

The way they figured it, with Christ out of the way, people would calm down, Rome would stay off their backs, and they could continue living in the style to which they'd grown accustomed. As Caiaphas suggested, it was a matter of third grade math: For the sake of many, it was better that one man die.

Interestingly enough, Christ reached the exact same conclusion. But he fulfilled Caiaphas' prophecy in a way Caiaphas never could have imagined.

See also: Matthew 23; John 12:24; Hebrews 10:14

WOE IS ME!

Woe to you, teachers of the law and Pharisees, you hypocrites! You are like whitewashed tombs, which look beautiful on the outside but on the inside are full of dead men's bones and everything unclean. In the same way, on the outside you appear to people as righteous but on the inside you are full of hypocrisy and wickedness.

MATTHEW 23:27–28

It would be nice to think Christ's words above were a scathing rebuke aimed solely at the religious stuffed shirts of his day. The way he laid into them, there's no question they were a dastardly bunch of pious old poops. But do his comments have other targets? Consider a sampling of his "Woe to you" charges:

"You travel over land and sea to win a single convert, and when he becomes one, you make him twice as much a son of hell as you are ... You give a tenth of your spices—mint, dill and cummin. But you have neglected the more important matters of the law—justice, mercy and faithfulness ... You clean the outside of the cup and dish, but inside they are full of greed and self-indulgence ... You snakes! You brood of vipers! How will you escape being condemned to hell?" (Matthew 23:15, 23, 25, 33)

Those were fighting words to the Pharisees, the particular Jewish sect which Christ singled out because of their extreme legalism and hypocrisy. But they didn't have a corner on the market of snooty pride or vile greed. The same traits Christ fingered are all around us—and in us—today.

Take a few minutes and identify examples of hypocrisy in the church—attitudes or actions which conflict with the Spirit of God as you know it:

_____

_____

_____

Finally, jot down any Pharisee-like qualities you find in yourself:

_____

_____

_____

See also: Luke 6:37–42; 12:1–5; 1 John 1:8–10

A BORN WINNER

> ***Don't you know that friendship with the world is hatred toward God? Anyone who chooses to be a friend of the world becomes an enemy of God.***
>
> ***JAMES 4:4***

Cindy was a living, breathing masterpiece. She was the prettiest girl I ever knew, the equal of any cover-girl model or actress. You name it: blond hair, blue eyes, a gorgeous tan, all the curves in all the right places. She not only stopped guys dead in their tracks, other girls even looked twice when she passed.

She was a shoo-in for homecoming queen and was the cheerleader everybody watched through binoculars. But she was more than a body. Cindy pulled straight A's in practically every class, earned honors in public-speaking competition, got elected to every school office she ever ran for, and had her choice of scholarship offers. She even lived in a nice house and had a pet dog that didn't shed. What more could anybody ask?

From time to time as the opportunity arose, I talked with Cindy about the Lord. I knew she was interested because she listened—*intently*. She even came right out and said she wanted to believe. But she always held back because she wasn't certain God wouldn't somehow ruin her life if she became a Christian. I think she secretly believed she might wake up ugly the next morning or contract some dreaded disease.

In the end, Cindy figured God needed her more than she needed him. And in that moment of decision, she fell for the lie of the devil, who whispered in her ear that she already had what really mattered—popularity, achievement, looks—and so why chance messing up a good thing by messing around with God-thoughts.

There's a reason Jesus said it's much easier for the poor and needy to enter his kingdom. A hungry, pregnant, fifteen-year-old girl living on a steam grate in New York and hustling quarters from passersby has no question about her needs. When you're at the bottom, things can only improve.

But Cindy, who had it so good already, feared things could only get worse. She essentially was right: hell loomed just around the corner.

See also: Matthew 5:3–10; 16:24–26; 19:24; 1 Timothy 6:6–10

MY FAVORITE TREE IS GONE

Then I saw a new heaven and a new earth, for the first heaven and the first earth had passed away, and there was no longer any sea. I saw the Holy City, the new Jerusalem, coming down out of heaven from God, prepared as a bride beautifully dressed for her husband. And I heard a loud voice from the throne saying, "Now the

dwelling of God is with men, and he will live with them.
They will be his people, and God himself will be with them
and be their God. He will wipe every tear from their eyes.
There will be no more death or mourning or crying or
pain, for the old order of things has passed away."

REVELATION 21:1–4

Jeff had a voice that was straight from heaven, and when he sang "The Lord's Prayer" at my wedding I had tears in my eyes. We were great friends all through high school and college. We surfed together, studied and prayed together, took weekend trips to the mountains together, and discussed first loves and future dreams together. As the scenario developed in our minds, he'd be a great lawyer, and I'd write the Great American Novel.

But then one day before the dreams had a chance to come true, Jeff noticed a little bump behind his ear. It seemed like nothing really, but he finally had it checked out—only to be told he had cancer . . . and six months to live.

Jeff is the first true friend I've lost. It's difficult to describe what it feels like afterward. It's sort of like having an awesome view of the Pacific Ocean—the cliffs and sweeping sands of La Jolla, the distant peaks of Catalina Island, and in the foreground a favorite shade tree. And then a building is constructed that partially blocks the view. I can stand in that same spot and look out where I used to see the beautiful evergreen, always full of birds, and my spirit falls.

Maybe the tree is still there, but it is hidden behind an impenetrable barrier. All I know is that I can't see it anymore.

I can stand there for hours, reminding myself of how the tree had balanced the view and given me so much pleasure. And I can optimistically think, It's *still* a gorgeous view. I can still see in the distance the breaking waves, the white sweeping sands, the gulls coasting on the wind, the faraway island peaks. Yes, it's still a gorgeous view. But the tree, my favorite tree, is gone.

That's how it feels.

Some days I'd give anything to be able to talk with him again. But I know he's happy where he is and wouldn't want to be back. Where he is now, every tear has been wiped from his eyes, and there is no more death or crying or pain. Where Jeff is now, he's healed.

Yet I still think of the view and the tree. I can't get it out of my mind. My favorite tree is gone.

See also: Isaiah 35; 65:17–25; 1 Corinthians 15:35–58

THE INSIDE STORY

These are written that you may believe that Jesus is the Christ, the Son of God, and that by believing you may have life in his name.

JOHN 20:31

As a journalist and author, I've had the opportunity to meet and interview many famous people. I've talked with Capitol Hillers, Hollyweirdos, Rock 'n' Rollers, and Super Bowlers.

If I want to know what the person is really like when they're not running (ruining?) the country, acting up a storm, blowing out eardrums, or making hamburger of other human beings, I don't just speak with the individuals themselves. For a well-rounded story, I spend time with their friends and associates as well. By utilizing other sources, I'm able to balance and interpret the quotes and material I get from the primary subject.

In trying to get to know more about Jesus Christ, the same methods apply. You must spend time reading what he said about himself—from his earliest recorded comments as a young boy (Luke 2:49), to his parting words before his ascension (Acts 1:7–8). A Bible which prints all of Christ's words in red is particularly helpful for this kind of study. But for a more fleshed-out look at who Christ is and how he behaved at the end of a long, hot day, you must turn to those who knew him best.

John was one of those people. A member of Christ's inner circle, John was probably his best friend. In his gospel, John skips over many of the basics about Christ's life (no blow-by-blow account of his birth, for example), because he figures you can get that elsewhere. Instead of focusing on the readily available facts, he interprets Jesus' life and ponders the meaning of what Jesus said and did as only a close friend can.

His words are full of reflection and commentary, and all for one express purpose: "That you may believe that Jesus is the Christ, the Son of God, and that by believing you may have life in his name" (John 20:31). In other words, he wants you to get to know Christ as well as he does, and thereby share eternity.

If you want the inside scoop on Jesus, spend a quiet evening this week with John.

See also: John 19:35; 1 John 1:1–3

GOOD-BYES

I have chosen you out of the world.

JOHN 15:19

I stood on the porch with my mother before me, my car behind me. The car was loaded down with all of my belongings and was riding low. I glanced at my watch. And then I looked up at my mother.

Her eyes were clouded, and there was a lone tear on her cheek. She didn't try to wipe it away, but just let it fall at her feet. There wasn't much that could be said, so she just opened her arms, and for several long moments we stood there holding each other and thinking about so many happy memories and how hard it was now

270

to say good-bye. I was moving five hundred miles away, and she knew what I didn't: that I wouldn't be back again, except to visit; and probably then with a wife.

"Good-bye, son," she said. Her eyes were wetter.

"Be sure to write," I managed. And then I squeezed the tears from my own eyes and walked to the car. A few moments later I was a set of taillights to her, and she was a distant, waving figure in my rearview mirror.

Good-bye is never an easy word. As far as words go, it ranks near the bottom of my list. At the top are such phrases as "Keep the change," "The exam's been canceled," and "Welcome home." Good-bye is in the dregs, along with "The basement's flooded," "I hope you're sitting down..." and "Call an ambulance."

"Good-bye" is a frequent word in the Christian's vocabulary because ultimately our roots and citizenship are in heaven. So we live as pilgrims, awaiting that still small voice of God that beckons, "Follow me." When it comes, we must be willing to leave family and friends and security behind, to live out of a duffel bag, to sleep anywhere but in our own bed—to say good-bye again and again and again.

For Christians, life is a journey that's homeward bound. And though on this side of eternity the partings don't become any easier, there is a bright side: Those who live in the Lord will never see each other for the last time.

See also: John 13:1; 18:36; Philippians 3:20; Colossians 3:1–3; 1 Peter 2:11–12

POINTS TO PONDER: ETERNITY

I tell you the truth, he who believes has everlasting life.

JOHN 6:47

The choices of time are binding in eternity.

JACK MACARTHUR

When you are with somebody you love, you have little if any sense of the passage of time, and you also have, in the fullest sense of the phrase, a good time. When you are with God, you have something like the same experience. The biblical term for the experience is Eternal Life. Another is Heaven.

FREDERICK BUECHNER

Faith is building on what you know is here, so you can reach what you know is there.

CULLEN HIGHTOWER

I thank Thee, O Lord, that Thou hast so set eternity within my heart that no earthly thing can ever satisfy me wholly.

JOHN BAILLIE

The average man does not know what to do with this life, yet wants another one which will last forever.

ANATOLE FRANCE

Eternity is not an everlasting flux of time, but time is a short parenthesis in a long period.

JOHN DONNE

The worst feeling in the world is the homesickness that comes over a man occasionally when he is at home.

ED HOWE

We think of Eternal Life, if we think of it at all, as what happens when life ends. We would do better to think of it as what happens when life begins.

FREDERICK BUECHNER

The thought of eternity consoles for the shortness of life.

LUC DE CLAPIERS

On earth there is no heaven, but there are pieces of it.

JULES RENARD

God, as Isaiah says "inhabiteth eternity" but stands with one foot in time. The part of time where he stands most particularly is Christ, and thus in Christ we catch a glimpse of what eternity is all about, what God is all about, and what we ourselves are all about, too.

FREDERICK BUECHNER

See also: Ecclesiastes 3:11; Isaiah 57:15; Mark 10:17–31; John 6:47

THE WAR WITHIN

> *"Come now, let us reason together," says the Lord. "Though your sins are like scarlet, they shall be as white as snow; though they are red as crimson, they shall be like wool."*
>
> ISAIAH 1:18

For as long as Andy could remember, there had been one very personal area of his life he didn't discuss with anybody. It was marked "Private—No Trespassing," and not even God could get through.

Andy prided himself on his openness in every other area of his life. It didn't bother him to talk about pride or greed or any other "safe sins." But that one private area of his life—that hidden corner of lust—was different. For Andy, lust dealt with fantasy thoughts and bewitching urges that were simply too personal to discuss with anybody.

Not wanting others to think he was some kind of Neanderthal lug, he kept his private lusts sealed off—only to have them fester and grow in the darkness. He soon graduated from the *Sports Illustrated* swimsuit issue to *Playboy*, and then to *Penthouse* and *Hustler*, and then to living a lie that extended beyond pictures in glossy magazines.

Andy was so concerned what people would think if they knew the true depths of his innermost thoughts that he maintained a thicker and thicker facade of outward spirituality. He was the first to quote a Bible verse, the first to pray, the first to share what God was doing in his life. He was the Christian whom others measured themselves by; the one whom parents wanted their daughters to marry.

But the mask eventually got too heavy, and before long Andy joined the list of Christian "has-beens." He just stopped coming to church and hanging around with other Christians. He began running with a faster crowd and drifting further and further and further from God. It didn't happen overnight, of course. Erosion of the heart is a slow process—so gradual that most of us hardly notice the problem.

But for Andy, as for anyone, that process began when he blocked off an area of his life as private; when he didn't seek God's help and cleansing forgiveness in *every* area of his life. Like Ananias and Sapphira (see Acts 5), he held something back.

The thing is, God wanted his whole heart. Not just a part—not even the biggest part. *All* of it. That's what Moses was getting at when he told the Israelites: "The Lord our God, the Lord is one. Love the Lord your God with all your heart and with all your soul and with all your strength" (Deuteronomy 6:4–5).

As Andy discovered, when you love God with less than all your heart, and when you keep him at a distance, God soon enough becomes a distant memory.

See also: Isaiah 1:18; Mark 2:17; Acts 24:16; James 4:8

THE WINNABLE WAR

> *Everything in the world—the cravings of sinful man, the lust of his eyes and the boasting of what he has and does—comes not from the Father but from the world. The world and its desires pass away, but the man who does the will of God lives forever.*

> 1 JOHN 2:16–17

It's not as if you plotted the evil; as if you woke up in the morning with some devious scheme contrary to God's plan for your life. It just sort of . . . well, *happened.*

It started innocently enough, as you were flipping through the latest issue of *Time*—a *news* magazine, for goodness' sake. Suddenly, you spot a picture of the latest lean teen queen, with her peek-a-boo blouse opened down to here and a come-hither look on her face that melts every good thought you've tried to think about the opposite sex. There is magic on the page, and you stare at the image until every curve is burned into your mind. There, safely tucked away, you fondle it mentally for hours.

Lust of the eye, as the Bible calls it, is not merely a guy's problem, consisting of leotards, bikinis, suggestive photographs, and lingerie ads in the Sunday paper. As the dictionary defines it, "lust is an overmastering desire or craving."

Thus, you can lust for popularity just as easily as you can lust for the latest lean teen queen. You can also lust for power and money and fame, as well as for a second helping of coconut cream pie, a red convertible, or Mr. Romeo's arms to hold you.

There is seldom anything wrong with the object of the lust itself. Women look the way they do because that's the way God designed them. Likewise, there is nothing inherently evil about money or cream pie or automobiles. Power, when channeled correctly, can create jobs and end wars. As for money, it is a necessary tool. It's the "love of money"—or the "lust" of money, the overmastering desire and craving for it—that the Bible decries.

As the verse above says, the cravings and lusts of sinful man come from the world. That is, they're fueled straight from hell. Presumably, that includes everything that promotes and encourages those cravings, such as the *Playboy* philosophy, the Miller Lite philosophy, or the Marlboro philosophy.

Until the Lord's promised return, we must wage a constant, internal war against these worldly desires. "In this world you will have trouble," Christ says in John 16:33. But, thankfully, he adds the clincher: "But take heart! I have overcome the world." In other words, it's a winnable war. Christ has set the enemy on his ear, and he's there to help you do the same in your very personal, daily struggles.

You can almost picture his open arms as he calls you close: "Come to me, all you who are weary and burdened, and I will give you rest" (Matthew 11:28).

See also: 2 Corinthians 7:1; James 4:4

FINDING RELIEF

Blessed are the pure in heart, for they will see God.

MATTHEW 5:8

Ever since Adam and Eve were booted out of Eden, there has been constant combat between the world in which we live and the kingdom of God. As you've been reading the past two days, that war is often waged in the innermost corners of our heart.

St. Augustine once described our condition here on earth as a simultaneous citizenship in two cities—the city of man and the City of God. Man's city is neon-lit, action-packed, lust-filled. It feels real and immediate. God's city is invisible and shrouded with mystery; some doubt whether it exists at all. Consequently, the whisper of the City of God is often overpowered by the siren call of the city of man.

What is the city of man, to be specific? The warm, intimate smile of Miss September is that city. As is lust in whatever form it takes. For you it may be the girl with the silky blouse opened a button too far; the lure of a buy-now, pay-later Visa card; the all-you-can-eat diner; a six-pack at a hot party; or the guy with expensive cologne and bedroom eyes who makes promises he can't keep for a night of love.

There are many good reasons for casting a deaf ear to the beckoning city of man and heeding the call of the City of God, but most of them sound extremely negative. People will tell you to be pure—or else you'll feel dreadfully guilty or die of AIDS or some such thing. There's truth to that, of course; short-term illicit pleasures generally do have long-term negative consequences, as any child of an alcoholic or coke-head can tell you.

But the best reason for seeking purity has nothing to do with the "live right, or else" rationale. Rather, it's the reason Christ gave in his Sermon on the Mount: "Blessed are the pure in heart, for they will see God."

Think about it: *The pure in heart will see God.* It's a staggering thought. But simply put, if you play by God's rules, he will reveal himself to you so that the City of God will become as real to you as the downtown skyline. Or to put it another way, you will be granted a glimpse of heaven right here on earth.

That promise may seem to lose its luster when compared with the warm glows and immediate thrills offered by Miss September or Mr. Romeo. But that's the deceiver whispering lies. The City of God is as real as the front of your face. And what you become as you build your citizenship in that city is far more inviting, fulfilling, and everlasting than if all your fantasies in the city of man were somehow fulfilled.

See also: Psalm 24:3–4; 73; John 10:10; Ephesians 3:14–21

BREAKING UP

Cast all your anxiety on him because he cares for you.

1 PETER 5:7

As soon as Kimberly picked up the phone, I knew we had problems. She sounded distant and tight. When I asked what was wrong, she didn't say anything. So I told her I'd drive over to talk about it.

"No, you'd better not," she hedged. There was a long, awkward silence. "Mike's here," she finally said.

"Mike?" I choked. "What—"

"Please, don't make this any harder than it already is," she said, and then for the next ten minutes she explained that she still loved me but wanted to start seeing other guys. Her words were like daggers, and when I hung up there were tears of pain in my eyes. Who was she fooling? She didn't still love me. Our relationship was over.

The first week was sheer torture. I tried to pray, but I found myself asking God to help Kimberly change her mind. I knew that was as futile as asking God to turn Mike into a duck, so instead I just prayed a single word: *hate*. Over and over I repeated that word to God because I couldn't see them together without burning up inside. After a couple of weeks, my rabid-dog feelings began to cool. I moved on to pray about *anger* and *revenge* and then *jealousy*.

Though praying didn't remove the hurt of breaking up, it kept the communication lines open with God and helped me reach the point where I could see Kimberly and Mike together without dwelling on breaking his knees. It also helped me see something else: just how much I had depended on another person for security—and how much more I needed to depend on God.

When my world began spinning out of control, my natural inclination was to focus on myself and my blur of emotions. With God's help, I learned to let him work things out inside of me—to be the still point of my turning world.

See also: Psalm 46:10; Philippians 4:6–7; James 5:13

LOVE TESTS

> *Test everything. Hold on to the good. Avoid every kind of evil.*

> 1 Thessalonians 5:21–22

When you're sick, you know it. It's a matter of taking your temperature or going to the doctor. Knowing when you're in love is a more confusing matter. There's no gauge to measure this most confusing of emotions. But in his book *I Married You*, Walter Trobisch provided the following practical tests to help you get a handle on love:

The sharing test. *Real love wants to share, to give, to reach out. It thinks of the other one, not of himself. When you read something, how often do you have the thought, I would like to share this with my friend? When you plan something, do you think of what you would like to do or what the other one would enjoy? . . .*

The strength test. *I got a letter once from a worried lover. He had read somewhere that one loses weight if one is truly in love. In spite of all his feelings of love, he didn't lose weight and that worried him. It is true that the love experience can also affect you physically. But in the long run, real love should not take away your strength; instead, it should give you new energy and strength. It should fill you with joy and make you creative, willing to accomplish even more . . .*

The respect test. *There is no real love without respect, without being able to look up to the other one. A girl may admire a boy when she watches him play soccer and score all the goals. But if she asks herself the question: "Do I want this boy to be the father of my children?" very often the answer will be in the negative. A boy may admire a girl when he sees her dancing. But if he asks himself the question: "Do I want this girl to be the mother of my children?" she may look very different to him.*

It would be easier, of course, if love could be determined as easily as measuring the air pressure in your tires. The above-mentioned guidelines may help you sort out your feelings. But in the end, you must rely on God to know best. You must also believe that he knows what is best and will help you decide "Who's the one" when the time is right.

See also: Psalm 37:4; 139:1–12; Jeremiah 29:11

THE CONFUSING EMOTION

Be imitators of God, therefore, as dearly loved children and live a life of love, just as Christ loved us and gave himself up for us as a fragrant offering and sacrifice to God. But among you there must not be even a hint of sexual immorality, or of any kind of impurity, or of greed, because these are improper for God's holy people.

EPHESIANS 5:1–3

Are you in love? There's more to this human emotion than mushy feelings, sweet dreams, and a rosy outlook on life whenever your "significant other" is in the vicinity. As you read yesterday, there are common-sense ways to test your feelings about love. Listed below are three more tests that Walter Trobisch provided in his book, *I Married You:*

The habit test. *Once a . . . girl who was engaged came to me and was very worried. "I love my fiancé very much," she said, "but I just can't stand the way he eats an apple" . . . Love accepts the other one with his habits. Don't marry on the installment plan, thinking that these things will change later on. Very likely they will not . . .*

The quarrel test. *When a couple come to me and want to get married, I always ask them if they have once had a real quarrel—not just a casual difference of opinion, but a real fight. Many times they will say, "Oh, no! Pastor, we love each other!" Then I tell them, "Quarrel first—and then I will marry you." The point is, of course, not the quarreling, but the ability to be reconciled to each other. This ability must be trained and tested before marriage . . .*

The time test. *A young couple came to me to be married. "How long have you known each other?" I asked. "Already three, almost four weeks," was the answer. This is too short. One year, I would say, is the minimum. Two years may be safer. It is also good to see each other . . . at work, in daily living, unshaved and in a T-shirt, or with hair that needs to be washed . . ., in situations of stress or danger."*

Trobisch made a final statement in his book. And that is: "Sex is no test of love . . . If a couple wants to use the sex act in order to know whether they love each other, one has to ask them, 'Do you love each other so little?'"

See also: John 13:34–35; 1 Corinthians 6:18–20

POINTS TO PONDER: THE OPPOSITE SEX

So God created man in his own image, in the image of God he created him; male and female he created them.

GENESIS 1:27

A person who despises or undervalues or neglects the opposite sex will soon need humanizing.

CHARLES SIMMONS

If all hearts were open and all desires known—as they would be if people showed their souls—how many gapings, sighings, clenched fists, knotted brows, broad grins, and red eyes would we see!

THOMAS HARDY

Where there is no God there is no man. Man without God is no longer man.

NICHOLAS BERDYAEV

The woman was formed out of man—not out of his head to rule over him; not out of his feet to be trod upon by him; but out of his side to be his equal, from beneath his arm to be protected, and from near his heart to be loved.

MATTHEW HENRY

All that I care to know is that a man is a human being—that is enough for me; he can't be any worse.

MARK TWAIN

There is a woman at the beginning of all great things.

ALPHONSE DE LAMARTINE

There are only two kinds of men: the righteous who believe themselves sinners; the rest, sinners who believe themselves righteous.

BLAISE PASCAL

Whatever women do, they must do twice as well as men to be thought half as good. Luckily, this is not difficult.

CHARLOTTE WHITTON

An honest man's the noblest work of God.

ALEXANDER POPE

It was Christ who discovered and emphasized the worth of woman. It was Christ who lifted her into equality with man. It was Christ who gave woman her chance, who saw her possibilities, who discovered her value.

ARTHUR JOHN GOSSIP

What a chimera, then, is man! What a novelty! What a monster, what a chaos, what a contradiction, what a prodigy! Judge of all things, feeble worm of the earth, depository of truth, a sink of uncertainty and error, the glory and the shame of the universe.

BLAISE PASCAL

You see, dear, it is not true that woman was made from man's rib; she was really made from his funny bone.

JAMES MATTHEW BARRIE

It is becoming more and more obvious that it is not starvation, not microbes, not cancer, but man himself who is mankind's greatest danger.

CARL GUSTAV JUNG

She is not made to be the admiration of all, but the happiness of one.

EDMUND BURKE

In short, the Man Jesus Christ has the decisive place in man's age-less relationship with God. He is what God means by "man," He is what man means by God.

J. S. WHALE

Man is always looking for someone to boast to; woman is always looking for a shoulder to put her head on.

H. L. MENCKEN

See also: Genesis 2:24–25; 3:1–24

THOSE WERE THE DAYS

You are my friends if you do what I command.

JOHN 15:14

The best time of year is June when an exam or two is all that stands before that big door opening onto a glorious summer. It's at that time yearbooks are distributed. These yearbooks record your year in pictures: the candid young-and-crazy times, the formal try-and-look-cool times, the big-smiling best of times, the eyes-closed worst of times.

What the camera doesn't capture, your friends do. They scribble comments in the margins of their pictures about the times you shared: "Remember when..." or "I'll never forget the time that ..." Maybe some say, "I wish we could have gotten to know each other better, but ..."

Consider for a moment that you've entered a sort of time warp. Instead of this being, well, *this* year, you're back in the year A.D. 18. And instead of attending your school, you're actually a student at Nazareth Prep Academy. One of your schoolmates, a graduating senior, is a young man named Jesus Christ. Your yearbooks have just been distributed, and you've exchanged yours with him.

Put yourself in his shoes for a few minutes. If you had the same relationship with him in person that you have with him now, what would he write about you? What would he remember about the past year and the times the two of you spent together? Were those times memorable? What would he say about your relationship? Were you close? Or were you always just passing each other in the halls, so to speak?

Take some time to write what you think *he* would write beneath his picture in your yearbook:

_____

_____

_____

_____

What do these comments say about your friendship? Are there ways you could improve your relationship?

See also: John 15:15; James 4:4

THE JUDGMENT

> *If, by the trespass of the one man, death reigned through that one man, how much more will those who receive God's abundant provision of grace and of the gift of righteousness reign in life through the one man, Jesus Christ.*

ROMANS 5:17

It was an open-and-shut case. The old man had been caught red-handed, heading out of the grocery store with a loaf of bread stuffed beneath his jacket. The facts were clear enough, and he even admitted his guilt. As he stood trembling before Judge LaGuardia in New York, he simply explained he stole the bread because his family was starving.

"Well, I have to punish you," Judge LaGuardia said. "The law makes no exception, and I have no choice but to fine you ten dollars."

The man swallowed hard, and his eyes grew moist. Where was he supposed to get that kind of money if he couldn't even afford a loaf of bread? The judge's sentence was beyond his ability to pay.

"The law is the law," he said curtly. But then the judge did something unexpected. He pulled out his wallet and extracted a bill. "But here's the ten dollars to pay for your fine.

"Furthermore," he said, tossing another dollar into his hat, "I am going to fine everyone in the courtroom fifty cents for living in a town where a man has to steal bread in order to eat." So he passed the hat up the aisle, and the old man, with the light of heaven in his eyes, left the courtroom with $47.50.

There's one word that describes the judge's action that day in New York: *grace*. Grace is when you get the opposite of what's deserved. It's the same word that describes God's action toward us. According to the laws of God, established from the foundation of the earth, the penalty of sin was death. And each of us, from Adam to ourselves and everybody else in between, has been caught red-handed. The law is the law, and the penalty had to be paid. But God did the unexpected. He paid the penalty himself. As Romans 5:8 says, "God demonstrates his own love for us in this: While we were still sinners, Christ died for us."

But he didn't stop there. As with the New York judge, he took matters one step further. He gave us a free gift of eternal life to boot.

It was a magnanimous act—so totally unexpected that the world hasn't gotten over it yet.

See also: Genesis 2:17; Romans 6:11–14, 23; Philippians 2:5–8

OPEN MY EYES, LORD

Why do you look at the speck of sawdust in your brother's eye and pay no attention to the plank in your own eye? How can you say to your brother, "Let me take the speck out of your eye," when all the time there is a plank in your own eye? You hypocrite, first take the plank out of your own eye, and then you will see clearly to remove the speck from your brother's eye.

MATTHEW 7:3–5

Open my eyes, Lord, that I may see . . .
My haste to say, "You are wrong,"
My hesitance to say, "I am to blame,"
My frowns when the other guy or other team wins,

My smiles when I cross the finish line first;
My 20/20 vision at finding cracks in others' character,
My halfhearted efforts to spot any flaws in myself.

Open my ears, Lord, that I may hear . . .
My laughter at the expense of others,
My cries when tables turn and the joke's on me;
My whoops when something awful happens to those I don't like,
My sighs when I'm the one who is kicked in the teeth;
My shouts when I detect sin in others,
My whispers when I am confessing my own sin.

Open my mind, Lord, that I may know . . .
My hardheadedness toward those who think I'm El Jerko,
My open-mindedness toward those who know I'm Mr. Right;
My recall of "place and time" when I've been wronged,
My forgetfulness of "when and how" I've hurt others;
My doubt that others have a snowball's chance of escaping hell,
My belief that I deserved heaven all along.

Open my heart, Lord, that I may feel . . .
My hatred of sin when others are doing the sinning,
My love of sin when it's my hand in the cookie jar;
My judgment of those whose skin or beliefs differ from mine,
My compassion toward those who are basically just like me;
My rejection of those with a smudge on their cheek,
My acceptance of myself, despite the mud on my face.

See also: Luke 6:37–38; Romans 14:10–13; 1 Corinthians 4:5

NEW BOUNDARIES

Be kind and compassionate to one another, forgiving each other, just as in Christ God forgave you.

EPHESIANS 4:32

It was another time and another place; during the early 1940s in France, to be exact. As Rita Snowden tells the story, some men carried the body of a dead friend to a church cemetery for burial. There they encountered unexpected problems.

The priest gently asked if their friend had been baptized in the Roman Catholic Church. When they said they weren't sure but figured he probably hadn't been, the priest said he unfortunately could not permit the burial in his churchyard. He apologized, but explained that rules were rules.

So the men sadly took their friend and buried him just outside the cemetery fence. It was dark when they finished the job, so they returned the following day to check on the grave. However, to their astonishment they could not locate it. Search as they might they could find no trace of the freshly dug soil.

Bewildered, they were about to leave when the priest approached and said he'd been troubled about not allowing their friend to be buried in the churchyard. So early in the morning he had risen from bed and *moved the fence* to include the body.

I think about that story whenever I get slighted in some awful way and feel tempted to seek revenge or shut the person out of my life. Perhaps you know the feeling: somebody wrongs you—blatantly—and you respond by erecting an emotional fence that leaves the person stranded and unforgiven on the other side.

That's a perfectly natural response. But what's natural and normal is not good enough in God's eyes. He would have you move the fence, just as he did for us. Even though we fell short of his standard by a country mile, God demonstrated his own love for us in this: "While we were still sinners, Christ died for us." That is, we deserved to be locked out of heaven, but Christ moved the barriers at Calvary.

Dwell on his supreme act of forgiveness today. And if there is somebody in your life who has done you wrong, ask God to help you forgive them, and thereby move the fence.

See also: Matthew 5:43–48; Romans 5:6–10

THE LONG SILENCE

We do not have a high priest who is unable to sympathize with our weaknesses, but we have one who has been tempted in every way, just as we are—yet was without sin.

HEBREWS 4:15

The following story by A. T. L. Armstrong is well-known, but I hope you'll agree it is worth retelling:

At the end of time, billions of people were scattered on a great plain before God's throne. Most shrank back from the brilliant light before them. But groups near the front talked heatedly—not with cringing shame, but with belligerence.

"How can God judge us? How can he know about suffering?" snapped a young woman, who jerked back a sleeve to reveal a tattooed number from a Nazi concentration camp. "We endured terror, beatings, torture, death!"

In another group, a young black man lowered his collar. "What about this?" he demanded, showing an ugly rope burn. "Lynched for no crime but being black! We have suffered in slave ships, been wrenched from loved ones, toiled till only death gave release."

Far out across the plain were hundreds of such groups. Each had a complaint against God for the evil and suffering he had permitted in his world. How lucky God was to live in heaven where there was no weeping, no fear, no hunger, no hatred. Indeed, what did God know of what man had endured in this world?

So each of these groups sent forth a leader, chosen because he had suffered most. There was a Jew, a black, an untouchable from India, an illegitimate, a horribly deformed arthritic, a victim of Hiroshima, and one from a Siberian prison camp. In the center of the plain, they consulted with each other.

At last they were ready to present their case. It was rather simple. Before God would be qualified to be their judge, he must endure what they had endured. Their decision was that God should be sentenced to live on earth—as a man!

But because he was God, they set certain safeguards to be sure he could not use his divine powers to help himself: Let him be born a Jew. Let the legitimacy of his birth be doubted, so that none will know who is really his father. Give him a work so difficult that even his family will snicker when he tries to do it. Let him try to describe what no man has ever seen, tasted, heard, or smelled. Let him try to describe God to man. Let him be betrayed by his dearest friends. Let him be indicted on false charges, tried before a prejudiced jury, convicted by a cowardly judge. At last, let him see what it means to be terribly alone, completely abandoned by every living thing. Let him be tortured, and then die!

When the list of conditions had been finalized, the thought seemed to strike all of the representatives at the same time. Slowly they backed away, and then disbanded altogether. They had no case. God, they realized, had already served the sentence.

See also: Romans 5:7–11; Philippians 2:8; 1 John 4:10–12

SEEKING AND SAVING

When Jesus heard what had happened, he with-drew by boat privately to a solitary place. Hearing of this, the crowds followed him on foot from the towns. When Jesus landed and saw a large crowd, he had compassion on them and healed their sick.

MATTHEW 14:13–14

Again and again throughout the Gospels, you read of Christ's compassion. When you come to a passage about him healing the sick, the blind, or the lame, it often is preceded with the statement: "He had compassion on them." Compassion is what motivated him to act.

Compassion has carried a divine flavor ever since. Compassion is, however, not the same thing as sympathy. Like pity, sympathy costs nothing and is worth nothing. Sympathy is the *thought* of love; compassion the *act*. When sympathy shrugs, "I might," compassion shouts, "*I will.*"

I can better illustrate the difference between the two by describing an incident that occurred when I took a wild adventure deep into South America. One night after pitching camp, three of us headed down to the banks of the Beni River to hunt alligators for dinner. But on the way I stepped into a mud-filled sinkhole. I whooped it up like a little kid—until I noticed that the once ankle-deep mud was covering my knees. By the time it reached my thighs I pictured myself as a target for a hungry alligator and began calling for help.

One of my friends ran up to my side and began pulling hard on my arm. Before long we were sinking side by side. I really started yelling for help then. Another of my friends ran up, calmly surveyed

295

our situation, then extended a thick branch that we grabbed and used to pull ourselves free.

That's the way it is with sympathy and compassion. Misery loves company, and a sympathetic person is quick to provide it—and soon sinks into the misery, too. A compassionate person works to *alleviate* trouble.

Thankfully, our Lord is filled with compassion toward us, rather than just sympathy. Compassion paved the way to heaven and got us saved; sympathy would merely have gotten us a consoling pat on the back.

See also: Isaiah 54:7–10; Matthew 15:29–38; 2 Corinthians 1:3–4

POINTS TO PONDER: COMPASSION

As God's chosen people, holy and dearly loved, clothe yourselves with compassion, kindness, humility, gentleness and patience.

COLOSSIANS 3:12

The dew of compassion is a tear.

LORD BYRON

The root of the matter is a very simple and old-fashioned thing, a thing so simple that I am almost ashamed to mention it for fear of the derisive smile with which wise cynics will greet my words. The thing I mean—please forgive me for mentioning it—is love. Christian love, or compassion.

BERTRAND RUSSELL

Tell me how much you know of the sufferings of your fellow men and I will tell you how much you have loved them.

HELMUT THIELICKE

The best portion of a good man's life is his little, nameless, unremembered acts of kindness and of love.

WILLIAM WORDSWORTH

Compassion is the sometimes fatal capacity for feeling what it's like to live inside somebody else's skin. It is the knowledge that there can never really be any peace and joy for me until there is peace and joy finally for you, too.

FREDERICK BUECHNER

If you quit loving the moment it becomes difficult, you never discover compassion.

DAVID AUGSBURGER

The value of compassion cannot be over-emphasized. Anyone can criticize. It takes a true believer to be compassionate. No greater burden can be borne by an individual than to know no one cares or understands.

ARTHUR H. STAINBACK

Compassion is the basis of all morality.

ARTHUR SCHOPENHAUER

Not a sigh is breathed, not a pain felt, not a grief pierces the soul, but the throb vibrates to the Father's heart.

ANONYMOUS

There is no exercise better for the heart than reaching down and lifting people up.

JOHN ANDREW HOLMER

When you are in trouble, people who call to sympathize are really looking for the particulars.

ED HOWE

Man may dismiss compassion from his heart, but God never will.

WILLIAM COWPER

Cleverness will enable a man to make a sermon, but only compassion for lost men will make him a soul winner.

LEONARD RAVENHILL

Should we feel at times disheartened and discouraged, a simple movement of heart toward God will renew our powers. Whatever he may demand of us, he will give us at the moment the strength and the courage we need.

FRANÇOIS DE SALIGNAC DE LA MOTHE FÉNELON

Our Lord does not care so much for the importance of our works as for the love with which they are done.

TERESA OF AVILA

See also: Isaiah 54:10; Zechariah 7:9–10; Mark 8:1–8

W E E K

24

IN GOOD HANDS

The Lord will go before you, the God of Israel will be your rear guard.

ISAIAH 52:12

When you're a senior in high school, you're supposed to feel invincible. Everybody says you have your whole life ahead of you and can be anything you want to be — even the president. Right. Then how come a simple little question from your aunt like, "By the way, what are you going to do next year?" causes a major panic attack?

Far from feeling invincible, you feel as if you're about to be swallowed by the great big world you're supposed to have by the tail. What are you going to do with your life? Marriage? College? Career? You haven't the foggiest, and that fact alone scares you to death.

While you can't know where the future will lead, God can because he has scouted up ahead. "The Lord will go before you," Isaiah says in the verse above. You need not worry. "For I know the plans I have for you," declares the Lord, "plans to prosper you and not to harm you, plans to give you hope and a future" (Jeremiah 29:11).

If that's not security enough, Isaiah also offers the assurance that God follows behind you: "The God of Israel will be your rear guard." This is military lingo. The Israelite army always had a vanguard and a rear guard. The vanguard preceded the soldiers and scouted unexplored territory. The rear guard followed behind, helping stragglers, and more or less picking up the pieces.

God does the same thing. He understands that you are sometimes hesitant to move forward because of past failures, bad memories, nagging sins, and old wounds. No problem. God follows behind, forgiving your sins, and helping you back on your feet. He picks up the pieces of your life, mending and restoring hurts and sorrows, and even creating positive results from negative incidents.

As the psalmist writes, "You hem me in, behind and before; you have laid your hand upon me. Such knowledge is too wonder-

300

ful for me, too lofty for me to attain" (Psalm 139:5–6). Indeed, God has a magnificent plan for your life that exceeds your wildest imaginings. And he's willing to both guide and guard you toward that destination. Why? He simply wants you to experience the "riches of his glory," which he has planned for you from the beginning of time.

See also: Deuteronomy 31:8; Ephesians 1:18–2:7

SURPRISE ENDINGS

> *No eye has seen, no ear has heard, no mind has conceived what God has prepared for those who love him.*
>
> 1 CORINTHIANS 2:9

As discussed yesterday, people are sometimes hesitant to draw closer to God and discover his unique plan for their lives because of past failures. Maybe you feel this way, too. Others may look at you and see a pretty decent Christian on the outside—but you know there's a monster lurking inside.

You know your innermost feelings and secret thoughts—thoughts that if flashed on a TV screen would send you running in embarrassment. Or perhaps you feel like you've let God down—not once or twice, but so many hundreds of times that you're beyond forgiveness. And now you're at the point where it seems that his magnificent plan for your life is but a mirage. Your life is full of regrets. Hounded by old wounds and bad memories, you think, "If only I had..."

If you think your life is shattered because of something you've done or neglected to do, consider Rahab. One of the more illustrious characters in the Bible, she is listed as being a key part of the family tree leading to Christ's birth (Matthew 1:5). And both the author of Hebrews (Hebrews 11:31) and the author of James (James 2:25) commend her for her great faith. Yet a peek at her resume in

Joshua 2 indicates that she was the first of the red-hot mamas, operating the best little whorehouse in Jericho.

Do you think she had regrets? Assuredly so. But she was smart enough that in her moment of greatest need, she turned toward God rather than turning away. And surprise of surprises: God welcomed her with open arms! It's the kind of "happily ever after" ending that makes you want to jump to your feet and applaud, to kick up your heels and holler, "Way to go, God!"

But save your applause for the grand finale. As the verse from 1 Corinthians above indicates, the Lord is saving the best for last. He's got a surprise up his sleeve that will boggle your most bizarre imaginings. It's a homecoming party reserved for those who, like Rahab, can quit stewing about the past and proceed to kick up their heels in the sunshine of God's love and forgiveness.

See also: Psalm 103; Romans 5:20

PLAIN EVERYDAY KINDNESS

Love is kind.

1 CORINTHIANS 13:4

I woke up this morning like I usually do, with my mouth feeling like a sweater and the rest of me feeling like a bad accident. I proceeded through my usual morning routine of showering and shaving and got to the point when I was just about to nick myself in the usual place on my chin when something rather nice happened. My wife quietly set a cup of coffee on the sink beside me, touched me gently on the arm, and then slipped away.

I don't know why that particular action made such an impression on me; my wife is normally pretty nice. But as I stood there with the razor poised to cut myself, it struck me that she didn't *have* to get me the coffee. I didn't even ask her to. Acting entirely on her own free will, she had chosen to be . . . well, kind. Not major kind, or automatic kind. Just plain everyday kind.

Early in our marriage we established a sort of rule that we would always try to be just plain everyday kind to each other. In the early years, however, we pretty much kept score. I knew when I was being kinder than she was, and she noticed when her acts of kindness went *un*noticed. But after a while, these everyday courtesies became a habit.

So now, if I'm in bed at night and my wife asks me to slip downstairs and turn off the cuckoo clock, I just get up and do it. I don't think much about it because the next day I might ask her to get me an aspirin from the medicine cabinet. I sometimes clean her hairbrush; she sometimes straightens my desk.

These are all things we could just as easily do for ourselves, and probably nine times out of ten we do. But by gladly doing them for each other, we demonstrate our love in very plain, ordinary ways. I can't help but think that has something to do with the fact that we're still married.

This isn't a particularly cosmic thought, I know. But this morning I experienced a small moment of unexpected kindness that set my day off. And in that moment I realized that kindness makes a difference.

See also: Matthew 20:25–28; 2 Corinthians 9:12–13

REACHING OUT

Always try to be kind to each other and to everyone else.

1 THESSALONIANS 5:15

I sometimes wonder if kindness isn't becoming as extinct as dinosaurs. That thought crossed my mind the other day when I pulled into what used to be called a "service" station for help, and the guy watching TV in the bullet-proof booth growled, "Sorry, no mechanics, only gas!"

All too often I feel like comedian Jay Leno, who says he once chided a supermarket clerk for failing to say thank you, only for her to snap back, "It's printed on your receipt!"

As discussed yesterday, a little kindness goes a long way. And the Bible indicates that plain everyday acts of kindness are noticed in heaven. Welcoming a little child or giving the weary a cup of cold water (Mark 9:37, 41), are specific acts commended by Christ.

Kindness means you smile. You look cheerful. You talk. It means you write an encouraging note on paper rather than just thinking about it in your head.

Kindness means sitting next to the new kid from Kentucky or offering your bus seat to the lady with three screaming kids. It's opening the door for your mom.

Kindness means listening to your grandmother tell the same story for the zeptillionth time, or laughing politely when your dad repeats his stale jokes for the zillyzeptillionth time. It's wishing your teacher a nice weekend.

Kindness means going the second mile, turning the other cheek, and loving people more than they deserve. It's not pretending you're asleep when your dad peeks in your room and wants to talk.

Kindness means opening your home to strangers and your heart to people who think, look, and act differently than you do. It's passing on a compliment, keeping a secret, and hushing up a rumor.

When you have more hassles in your day than hours, it's easy for kindness to get lost in the squeeze. When faced with stress, most people stay close to home base, worrying about their own concerns before thinking about making somebody else's day. It takes time and effort to be kind. And it's usually not convenient.

But that's what kindness is all about. It's being willing to take the time and give the effort—even when inconvenient. And at the end of your life, you can say you've lived well if you've been generous with those "little, nameless, unremembered acts of kindness" (Wordsworth). You might even go so far as to think of them as stepping-stones toward heaven.

See also: Acts 20:35; 1 Peter 3:8–9

AGAINST THE WALL

A cheerful heart is good medicine, but a crushed spirit dries up the bones.

PROVERBS 17:22

Whenever I'm faced with tough times or a gut-deep case of the gloomies, I find hope in the following story by G. W. Target. Place a copy in your locker or on your bathroom mirror. Or pass it along to a friend who is struggling.

There were once two men, both seriously ill, in the same small room of a great hospital. Quite a small room, it had one window looking out on the world.

One of the men, as part of his treatment, was allowed to sit up in bed for an hour in the afternoon (something to do with draining the fluid from his lungs). His bed was next to the window. But the other man had to spend all his time flat on his back.

Every afternoon when the man next to the window was propped up for his hour, he would pass the time by describing what he could see outside. The window apparently overlooked a park where there was a lake. There were ducks and swans in the lake, and children came to throw them bread and sail model boats. Young lovers walked hand in hand beneath the trees, and there were flowers and stretches of grass, games of softball. And at the back, behind the fringe of trees, was a fine view of the city skyline.

The man on his back would listen to the other man describe all of this, enjoying every minute. He heard how a child nearly fell into the lake, and how beautiful the girls were in their summer dresses. His friend's descriptions eventually made him feel he could almost see what was happening outside.

Then one fine afternoon, the thought struck him: Why should the man next to the window have all the pleasure of seeing what was going on? Why shouldn't he get the chance? He felt ashamed, but the more he tried not to think like that, the worse he wanted a change. He'd do anything!

One night as he stared at the ceiling, the other man suddenly woke up, coughing and choking, his hands groping for the button that would bring the nurse running. But the man watched without moving—even when the sound of breathing stopped. In the morning, the nurse found the other man dead, and quietly took his body away.

As soon as it seemed decent, the man asked if he could be switched to the bed next to the window. And they moved him, tucked him in, and made him quite comfortable. The minute they'd gone, he propped himself up on one elbow, painfully and laboriously, and looked out the window.

It faced a blank wall.

I've known people whose lives have "faced a blank wall"—of tight finances, intense pain, or a broken family—yet they somehow managed to convey hope and joy to those around them. Their joy was not dependent on circumstances, but on the Lord. As Nehemiah wrote, "The joy of the Lord is your strength" (Nehemiah 8:10). Indeed, joy is soul deep. And if you know the Lord, it should be evidenced in your life . . . even when there is nothing to smile about.

See also: Habakkuk 3:17–19; 1 Thessalonians 5:16–18

SERIOUS BUSINESS

May the God of hope fill you with all joy and peace as you trust in him, so that you may overflow with hope by the power of the Holy Spirit.

ROMANS 15:13

One of my best friends in high school didn't want to become a Christian for one main reason. It wasn't that she didn't believe in God; she basically did. But she had this fear that he would take away all her fun. For her, life was a party. And her gut feeling about God was that he was something of a party pooper. At least that's the impression she got from most of the Christians she knew.

Over and over she heard the testimonies of how new Christians had given up things like booze and cigarettes and sex. Some had even quit dancing and going to movies. But if you asked her, they also seemed to have sworn off smiling and laughing and having genuine stand-up-and-holler good-old-times. She had one word which described the whole bunch: boring. It was a broad generalization, to be sure. But it came close to the mark.

Jesus had similar complaints about the religious people of his day. The synagogues were filled with stuffy starched-togas who thought they knew all about God but didn't know a thing about living or laughing. On days of fasting, they assumed the personality of soggy oatmeal and advertised their holiness by moaning and groaning on street corners.

Holiness was important to Christ, but so was happiness. And if you take his life as an example, you see that the two characteristics are not mutually exclusive. Having one doesn't mean you can't have the other. It simply cannot be said that during his time on earth Christ didn't enjoy kicking up his heels a little. He liked parties and fun and swarms of kids—and it was for these things that the sour-puss Pharisees criticized him most.

Christ was a storyteller, and the tales he spun were often of joyous feasts and celebrations. He wanted people to know that heaven was not something to dread, but something to look forward to, something that ought to get your blood pumping with excitement. In fact, he likened the kingdom of God to a rollicking banquet and a wedding feast—tremendously happy, joyous occasions. His first miracle, that of turning water into wine, was done for the pure, unadulterated pleasure of those around him.

Isaiah may have described Christ as being "a man of sorrows, and familiar with suffering" (Isaiah 53:3), but that doesn't mean he was a stranger to joy and happiness. And there's every indication that he's preparing a major, foot-stomping bash for his children in heaven. Indeed, joy is serious business with Christ. And if you seek to be conformed to his image, you might consider kicking up your heels and shouting "Whoopee!" at least once before the day is out. Twice, if you mean it.

See also: 1 Corinthians 2:9; Hebrews 12:2

POINTS TO PONDER: JOY AND HAPPINESS

If you obey my commands, you will remain in my love, just as I have obeyed my Father's commands and remain in his love. I have told you this so that my joy may be in you and that your joy may be complete.

JOHN 15:10–11

What I am anxious to see in Christian believers is a beautiful paradox. I want to see in them the joy of finding God while at the same time they are blessedly pursuing him. I want to see in them the great joy of having God and yet always wanting him.

A. W. TOZER

The moments of happiness we enjoy take us by surprise. It is not that we seize them, but that they seize us.

ASHLEY MONTAGUE

Be happy while you're living, for you're a long time dead.

SCOTTISH PROVERB

It is an illusion to think that more comfort means more happiness. Happiness comes of the capacity to feel deeply, to enjoy simply, to think freely, to be needed.

STORM JAMESON

You cannot read the Gospels without seeing that Jesus did not tell men how to be good in the manner of the moralists of every age, he told them how to be happy.

SIR THOMAS TAYLOR

This is the secret of joy. We shall no longer strive for our own way; but commit ourselves, easily and simply, to God's way, acquiesce in his will and in so doing find our peace.

EVELYN UNDERHILL

There is no happiness for people at the expense of other people.

ANWAR EL-SADAT

Happiness makes up in height for what it lacks in length.

ROBERT FROST

We hold these truths to be self-evident: that all men are created equal; that they are endowed by their Creator with certain inalienable Rights; that among these are Life, Liberty and the pursuit of Happiness.

THE DECLARATION OF INDEPENDENCE

A "right to happiness" ... sounds to me as odd as a right to good luck. For I believe—whatever one school of moralists may say—that we depend for a very great deal of our happiness or misery on circumstances outside all human control. A right to happiness doesn't, for me, make much more sense than a right to be six feet tall, or to have a millionaire for your father, or to get good weather whenever you want to have a picnic.

C. S. LEWIS

The foolish man seeks happiness in the distance, the wise grows it under his feet.

JAMES OPPENHEIM

One summer night, out on a flat headland, all but surrounded by the waters of the bay, the horizons were remote and distant rims on the edge of space. Millions of stars blazed in darkness, and on the far shore a few lights burned in cottages. Otherwise there was no reminder of human life. My companion and I were alone with the stars: the misty river of the Milky Way flowing across the sky, the patterns of the constellations standing out bright and clear, a blazing planet low on the horizon. It occurred to me that if this were a sight that could be seen only once in a century, this little headland would be thronged with spectators. But it can be seen many scores of nights in any year, and so the lights burned in the cottages and the inhabitants probably gave not a thought to the beauty overhead; and because they could see it almost any night, perhaps they never will.

RACHEL CARSON

That man is the richest whose pleasures are the cheapest.

HENRY DAVID THOREAU

There are joys which long to be ours. God sends ten thousand truths, which come about us like birds seeking inlet; but we are shut up to them, and so they bring us nothing, but sit and sing awhile upon the roof, and then fly away.

HENRY WARD BEECHER

May we never let the things we can't have, or don't have, or shouldn't have, spoil our enjoyment of the things we do have and can have. As we value our happiness let us not forget it, for one of the greatest lessons in life is learning to be happy without the things we cannot or should not have.

RICHARD L. EVANS

See also: Psalm 30:4–5; Ecclesiastes 2:26; 1 Thessalonians 5:16–18

WEEK

25

LAWS OF THE LAND

I have chosen the way of truth; I have set my heart on your laws. I hold fast to your statutes, O Lord; do not let me be put to shame. I run in the path of your commands, for you have set my heart free.

PSALM 119:30–32

We all know about laws such as those that prohibit us from running red lights or having target practice on a downtown street or disrobing in public. But there are some amazing regulations still on the books that might not be so familiar.

For instance, did you know that you cannot make ugly faces at anyone in Zion City, Illinois, bite your landlord in Rumford, Maine, or mistreat a rat in Denver? Not to mention that you can't wear a false mustache in an Alabama church if it's likely to make people laugh, or grow a real one in Indiana if you are one who "habitually kisses human beings."

In San Jose, California, it is still illegal to sleep in your neighbor's outhouse without his permission. It's also illegal to hang men's and women's underwear on the same clothesline in Minnesota, to spit on your laundry in San Francisco, or to tickle a girl under the chin with a feather duster in Portland, Maine.

Though these laws remain in the various penal codes, we recognize how silly and outmoded they are. Yet we often perpetuate other nonsensical laws in our society—laws that are regularly adhered to though they are not formally recognized.

For instance, we still subscribe to the unwritten law that people are valued more for what they are (good-looking, talented, bright) rather than for who they are in God's eyes (unique creations whom he loves infinitely). In a similar fashion, we undervalue the outcast, the handicapped, the poor—the very people to whom Christ devoted special time and attention.

An additional belief we often hold is that success is determined by the size of your bank account, the worth of your car, the prestige of your job—though in God's eyes these are all nonessentials that you can spend your whole life seeking, only to lose your soul in the process.

Someday ... yes, someday we will recognize that these unwritten laws are as silly as those which forbid you to swim on dry land in Santa Ana, California, hunt ducks from an airplane in Colorado, or punch a bull in the nose in Washington, D. C.

See also: Psalm 146; Matthew 5:3–10; 6:19–21; Luke 12:13–34

GET OFF MY BACK!

There will be terrible times in the last days. People will be lovers of themselves, lovers of money, boastful, proud, abusive, disobedient to their parents, ungrateful, unholy.

2 TIMOTHY 3:1–2

It's been said that you should treat your parents with all the respect, patience, and understanding you'd show a friend. Tim Stafford figured that's how he'd always treated them, but then he had a little daydream. What if his best friend came over, and he treated him like he commonly treated his parents ...

"Hi," Ernie said. "Are you ready to go to the basketball game?"

"Would you get off my back?" I said in my most exasperated tone. "What difference does it make if we're a little late?"

"None, I guess. What did you do this afternoon?"

"Nothing," I grunted.

"Did you have practice after school?"

"Nah."

"So what did you do?"

"Why do you always pry into my private life?" I exploded.

"Sorry," Ernie said. He looked a little hurt and tried to change the subject. "Hey, I saw you talking to Charlotte today. How do you rate? She's really something, isn't she?"

"Look, I can't see that it's any of your business."

"Hey, I was just trying to ... Aw, forget it. Let's go."

"Can I have five bucks?" I asked.

"Well, I don't know," Ernie said doubtfully. "I don't have much money. Don't you have any money of your own?"

"Where would I get it?" I asked sarcastically. "I suppose you want me to get a job on top of everything else I do."

"Who said anything about a job?"

"Everybody always wants you to get terrific grades and practically be an Einstein, but they won't loan you the money to go to a basketball game and relax once in a while. I suppose you'd prefer I went out drinking. That's cheaper, you know."

"Forget I said anything," Ernie said. "You can have the money. Let's just go to the game. We're late already."

"You're always pushing me," I grumbled on the way out the door. But I stopped. "Ernie, do we have to go in that crummy car? It looks so old. Everybody else drives a new car, and I have to go in that beat-up refugee from a junkyard. Can't you get something new?"

"I would if I had the money," Ernie mumbled.

"That's the trouble with you," I said. "All you think about is money. You're so tied up in cash that you don't take time to think about what's important to the rest of us."

"Yeah, right," Ernie said, his head down.

"You bet I'm right," I said. "And if you think I'm going to sit with you at the game, you're crazy!"

See also: Proverbs 15:20; 20:20; 23:25; Ephesians 6:1–2; Colossians 3:20

PERSONAL CONCERN

You shall not misuse the name of the Lord your God, for the Lord will not hold anyone guiltless who misuses his name.

EXODUS 20:7

I was one hundred miles out to sea, trying to hook up with a school of halibut making their way from Japan. But it looked like there would be no fishing because, despite the zeptillion gallons of ocean all around me, there didn't appear to be any fish. And so after a couple of hours I lay back and tried to do something worthwhile, like work on my tan.

I was drifting off to never-never land when all of a sudden a crew member screamed, "Look up!" at the top of his lungs. The engine was cut, and as the boat coasted into the middle of a school of fish, everybody raced for the bait tank and then flung their lines overboard.

Moments later, even as I was grabbing for a bait fish, one of the fishermen bellowed excitedly, "Jesus Christ, I hooked a whale!"

I've been around enough to know people don't mean anything by using Christ's name in that way. He might just as well have said, "Wow!" or "Man alive!" or some other such phrase to convey his excitement. But he didn't.

Upon hearing the name of Christ shouted across the ocean like that, I immediately looked up. It was like the way I react when I hear somebody calling the name of a good friend across the parking lot—I glance up, scan the aisles of cars, and half expect to see my friend standing nearby—but more often than not, the person is calling somebody else. I had that same reaction that day out at sea. It was almost as if I expected Christ to be standing right there. I take the name Jesus Christ that personally.

317

I thought about saying something to the man, but let it pass—until a short time later when he GD'd up a storm after accidentally snagging his finger on the tip of the hook. I walked over, told him I was sorry about his finger, but then said something to the effect of, "Contrary to popular belief, God's last name is not Damn."

People use his name without really thinking about it, and maybe that's the problem. God is picky about how his name is used, and he doesn't want it profaned by loose usage. He wants you to think about it, to ponder it. His is a holy name—a name the Bible says should cause every person to worship him: "At the name of Jesus every knee should bow, in heaven and on earth and under the earth, and every tongue confess that Jesus Christ is Lord" (Philippians 2:10–11).

Right now people have a choice in that matter. Ultimately, however, all people will worship him as Lord—whether willingly or not: "'As surely as I live,' says the Lord, 'every knee will bow before me; every tongue will confess to God'" (Romans 14:11).

I think it's important to remind people about that from time to time.

See also: Leviticus 19:12; Ezekiel 39:7; Matthew 5:33–37; Philippians 2:10

LOVING GOD

You see, at just the right time, when we were still powerless, Christ died for the ungodly. Very rarely will anyone die for a righteous man, though for a good man someone might possibly dare to die. But God demonstrates his own love for us in this: While we were still sinners, Christ died for us.

ROMANS 5:6–8

"If" love is conditional. It says I love you, Lord ...
if you get my parents off my back;
if you give me the inside track with the babe of my dreams;
if you do something about my boss;
if you cure my acne;
if you get me accepted to the college of my choice;
if you arrange my life like I feel it ought to be arranged.

"Because" love is easy love. It says I love you, Lord ...
because I just got a pay raise and can finally start living;
because I aced an exam I didn't even study for;
because my car repair bill was only $57.60;
because things are looking good with Blue Eyes;
because my creep brother actually got saved;
because things are basically going well for me right now.

"Anyhow" love is hard, unconditional love. It says I love you,
      Lord ...
anyhow, even if the lab tests are positive;
anyhow, even when the only person I can talk to moves away;
anyhow, even though people die because of hunger and war;
anyhow, even if Grandpa doesn't make it through the night;
anyhow, even when you don't answer my prayers like I want;
anyhow, even when my life is crumbling and you feel distant;

      Lord, I desperately want to love you *anyhow*, with no strings attached ... because that's how you love me. I am trying, honestly trying, to learn to love and worship you the same way.

See also: Mark 12:28–30; John 14:15; 1 John 2:3–6

319

MAYBE NEXT WEEK

> *Let us not give up meeting together, as some are in the habit of doing, but let us encourage one another – and all the more as you see the Day approaching.*

HEBREWS 10:25

Lord, I keep telling myself I need to go to church more, but after a whole week of racing around mornings to get ready for school, and then having to show up for work at the crack of dawn Saturday ... well, Sunday is the one day of the week I've got to sleep in. You don't mind if I take a little break, do you? Just this Sunday?

You're an understanding God, right? One who knows that church is just another item on my pressure-cooker list of things to do. I'm fifty pages behind the class in history, I've got a five-pager to write for English, and I'm looking down the barrel at a big test in biology. Not to mention that my mom's hounding me to paint the fence, my radiator needs flushing, and my girlfriend hasn't been called in two days. No offense, Lord, but I just don't think my schedule can handle any additional strain.

I'm not making excuses here, but ... I don't think I *can* get out of bed. After last night's party, there's this feeling I have of train whistles blowing in my head. If Sunday morning came at any other time of the week, I could probably cope with it. But it comes so early after Saturday night, which is the one night I can stay out late and have a good time and ... oh, my aching head!

Okay, Lord, I'm getting up. See? The covers are off and my right foot is touching the ground. Maybe with a couple of aspirin I can make it through the service without falling out of the pew and grabbing my head. There, now, both feet are ... *Yawn!* ... on the ground, and ... *Stretch!* ... Give me just five more minutes to sleep, and then ...

Lord, I must have overslept! Oh, no—it's already 10:05 and I've missed church! Well, not exactly. There's always the second service, but I probably wouldn't know anybody. And then there's the matter of the playoffs starting in just a couple hours, which is just enough time to shower and eat and . . .

Lord, maybe things will be different next week. Yeah, maybe.

See also: Genesis 2:2–3; Matthew 18:20; Acts 2:42

TOP SECRET

> *Keep watch, because you do not know on what day your Lord will come.*
>
> Matthew 24:42

The world stopped to listen a few years ago when Chicago's mayor announced plans to move into the city's Cabrini Green housing projects. It seemed like a nutty thing to do.

The high-rise neighborhood is a virtual hell on earth—a world where thirteen-year-olds tuck sawed-off shotguns beneath their beds at night; a world where if you don't join a gang, you mortgage your life for "protection"; a world where court cases are regularly dropped because witnesses suddenly "forget" what they saw or mysteriously "disappear"; a neighborhood where you wouldn't take your dog for a walk—if you cared for the dog.

The mayor wanted to establish peace in the neighborhood once and for all by moving in. Reporters around the world wanted to know the date of the move, but calls were not returned. Repairmen, police, exterminators—everyone sought information about when the mayor would arrive so they could prepare, get things polished up, put their best foot forward. But the mayor stonewalled.

"My arrival will be a secret. No one will know until I'm there," the mayor said, not wanting people to start cleaning things up the day before. Without a move-in date, there would be daily anticipation. Everybody would have a better quality of life if The Day could happen any old day.

And so it was some 2,000 years ago when Christ promised to return to earth, but declined to say exactly when. Had he pinpointed the date, people would have circled it in red on their calendars and then ducked into church the day before to repent.

But nobody knows the hour or the day of his arrival. He intended that we live each day as if his arrival were imminent. He wants to be greeted by saints, not whitewashed pretenders.

See also: Matthew 24:37–44; 25:1–13

POINTS TO PONDER: WORSHIP

Come, let us bow down in worship, let us kneel before the Lord our Maker; for he is our God and we are the people of his pasture, the flock under his care. Today, if you hear his voice, do not harden your hearts.

PSALM 95:6–8

It cannot be that the instinct which has led to the erection of cathedrals, and of churches in every village, is wholly mistaken and misleading. There must be some great truth underlying the instinct for worship.

SIR OLIVER LODGE

Measure not men by Sundays, without regarding what they do all the week after.

THOMAS FULLER

Rejoice in him and make a fool of yourself for him the way lovers have always made fools of themselves for the one they love. A Quaker Meeting, a Pontifical High Mass, the Family Service at

First Presbyterian, a Holy Roller Happening—unless there is an element of joy and foolishness in the proceedings, the time would be better spent doing something useful.

FREDERICK BUECHNER

When Christian worship is dull and joyless, Jesus Christ has been left outside—that is the only possible explanation.

JAMES S. STEWART

The glory of God is a living man; and the life of man consists in beholding God.

ST. IRENAEUS

O my Lord! If I worship Thee from fear of hell, burn me in hell, and if I worship Thee from hope of Paradise, exclude me from it; but if I worship Thee for Thine own sake, then withhold not from me Thine Eternal Beauty.

RABIA AL-ADAWIYYA

It is only when men begin to worship that they begin to grow.

CALVIN COOLIDGE

Many of today's young people have little difficulty believing that God was in Christ. What they find hard to accept is that Christ is in the church.

ERNEST T. CAMPBELL

As you worship, so you serve.

THOMAS L. JOHNS

To worship God means to serve him.

FREDERICK BUECHNER

Some people in church look like guests at a royal banquet, who couldn't afford to be left out, but have been forbidden by their doctor to eat anything.

W. R. MALTBIE

The true inner life is no strange or new thing; it is the ancient and true worship of God, the Christian life in its beauty and in its own peculiar form. Wherever there is a man who fears God and lives the good life, in any country under the sun, God is there, loving him, and so I love him too.

GERHARD TERSTEEGEN

See also: 1 Chronicles 16:29; Luke 4:5–8; John 4:23–24

The Best Devotions for Teens

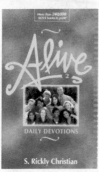